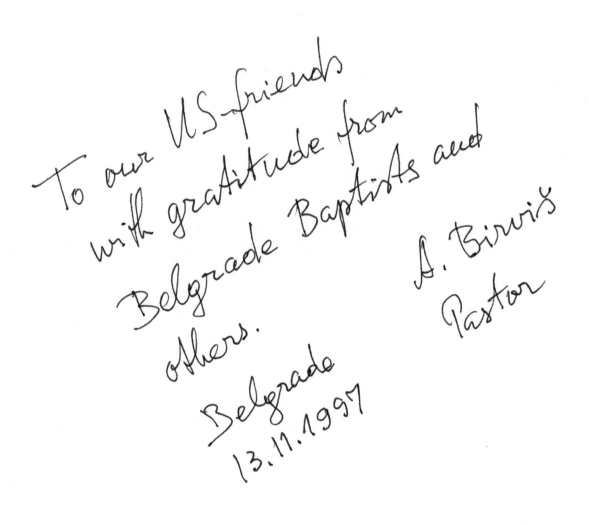

To our US-friends
with gratitude from
Belgrade Baptists and
others.
Belgrade
13.11.1997

A. Birvis
Pastor

YUGOSLAVIA

© For co-publishers »Mladinska knjiga« International
Ljubljana, 1982.

Publisher:
SVJETLOST
Sarajevo

For the publisher:
Gavrilo GRAHOVAC

Editor:
Mirza FILIPOVIĆ

Translation:
Milan MLAČNIK

Design:
Tadej TOZON

Printing and binding Mladinska knjiga, Ljubljana – 1990

ISBN 86-01-01766-5

CIP – Katalogizacija u publikaciji
Narodna i univerzitetska biblioteka Bosne i Hercegovine, Sarajevo

UDK 908(497.1)(084.1)

    YUGOSLAVIA / [translation Milan Mlačnik ; photographs Vilko Zuber ... et al.]. – Sarajevo :
Svjetlost, 1990. – 263 str. : ilustr. ; 30 cm

ISBN 86-01-01766-5

YUGOSLAVIA

SVJETLOST

SARAJEVO 1990

Contents

Nature – Contrasts and Highlights

Footprints of Time

Gem-Like Townscapes

Treasure-Houses

Traditions

Landmarks

Tokens of Revolution

Capitals

Note: Unless stated otherwise, the captions follow
from left to right and from top to bottom.

Foreword

A STEPPING-STONE TO WONDERFUL YUGOSLAVIA

After the battle of Troy, Ulysses chose a rather devious route home. Historians cannot quite make up their minds whether the gods should be praised or blamed for that. In any case, he spent no less than seven years in the embrace of the nymph Calypso, on an Adriatic island where Nature was not niggardly of other charms either.

Ulysses was neither the first nor the last traveller charmed by the little stretch of land today called Yugoslavia, dazzled by the heirlooms of her past, overawed by the exploits of her more recent history. For the benefit of the questioning armchair traveller a figurative bridge towards the country's hills and valleys, joys and sorrows has been lately erected by Nobel prize winner Ivo Andrić, in the guise of his novel "Bridge on the Drina". A bridge is, indeed, a fitting symbol for this country, which looms far larger in the news than it actually is. A bridge, a unique, even spectacular passage between two worlds, both separating and joining them, and at the same time leaving some room for reveries.

In this tract of what is often pictured as "wild Balkans", Christ sees eye to eye with Allah, East and West shake hands, practical-minded Europe indulgently smiles at the spirituality of the near and far South, words in half a dozen languages sound alike, and the snows of Alpine peaks are mirrored in the warm Mediterranean. The peace and balance the country currently enjoys are by no means an expression of youthful dash, but rather a reflection of the wisdom of ripe age, acquired at the price of shattering experiences. But words are rather feeble instruments to grapple with life, and a book is unequal to the task of conjuring up a world of beauty. Yet we venture to offer you a work compiled by several authors, who have joined their forces to attempt the impossible. Our YUGOSLAVIA presents the would-be traveller with a handful of pearls, which he can thread into a necklace according to his own taste, by working out his route for himself.

He might, for instance, start out from Dubrovnik, the "princess of the Adriatic", the city that opened Europe's first pharmacy back in the Dark Ages, and sported a theatre before Shakespeare was even born. He might choose Korčula for his first port of call, the island where the ancestral home of the Polo family will remind him of the most famed of the medieval wayfarers. From there he may stray northwards, all the way to Ribnica, whose tradesmen were granted the monopoly of peddling their woodware throughout Europe as early as 1492, or he might swerve southwards, to Rijeka Crnojevića, where the first book in Cyrillic script was printed a year later. He may end up in Belgrade, at the grave of the man whose funeral was the occasion for the greatest gathering of statesmen this century has ever seen.

Everywhere he strays, the wanderer will be greeted by a proudly smiling Nature. She is well aware she hides Europe's most staggeringly beautiful river, mightiest caves, deepest canyon; more than a thousand stony or sandy islands; the largest lakes of the Balkans; several thousand animal species, some of them thirty million years old; some of the old continent's last virgin forests, the refuge of a number of rare mammals; and marshlands that serve as stopovers to countless winged migrants in search of sunshine. The stony desert of the Karst has given birth to the fabulous white horse, the Lipizzaner, and the sandy beaches far to the south nurture a 2500-year-old olive-tree. In places the earth has laid bare her strata, to disclose the remnants of primitive man, whom she had already inspired, as the sculptures of Lepenski Vir testify, to capture beauty into stone.

Beauty has continually changed her aspect here. To show man a foretaste of paradise, she has taken her abode in churches and monasteries, where she shines from Byzantine frescos and carvings, and ogles from Gothic sculptures and murals. She has conjured up one of the world's finest collections of icons; but deciding that man was, after all, a down-to-earth being, she has also guided the heavy peasant hands of the naive painters of Hlebine.

The traveller will discover at every step that his predecessors of centuries ago or only a few decades since did not always come with the best intentions. But the locals have always been pretty touchy about their independence, and have spared no pains to regain or preserve it. It is impossible to miss the ubiquitous memorials of their sacrifices. You will find the roadsides lined with white tombstones, "stećaks" or "krajputaši", and decaying wooden crosses, a ghost army haunting the battlefields of eternal peace. You will, no doubt, shudder at the skulls of rebels embedded in the Ćele Kula, the "Tower of Skulls". You may even stray into one of the "school classes" held at the mass cemetery of the 300 schoolchildren and 7000 adults executed in Kragujevac, and share, with Jean-Paul Sartre, the "experience of the pain of a whole nation".

A rebellious spirit has smouldered here throughout recorded history, flaming up in the medieval peasant revolts, the first republic of the Balkans about the turn of our century, or the Partisan fighting of World War II. The painstakingly preserved ancient customs and habits, the lovingly penned ancient manuscripts, the sonorous folk poetry — they all reflect the exuberance and pride of a people determined to preserve its own ways at all costs.

This fierce determination to live her own pattern of life in absolute independence is, indeed, the secret mainspring of Wonderful Yugoslavia, small as countries go, yet big in her own way.

The native country occasionally forgets one or other of her children. But good children never forget their birthplace. This book on YUGOSLAVIA, a mosaic of hundred-odd articles grouped in ten-odd chapters, will offer you one of the possible explanations why one can love this country.

At the same time it is a hearty invitation to every modern would-be Ulysses to venture a step across her threshold, to yield to her charms — and perhaps to grope his way towards his own happiness.

Slavko Pregl

Nature – Contrasts and Highlights

Beauty highlighted by contrast, contrast underscored by beauty — and all a magnificent spectacle of Nature's creativity. Or rather — all a single huge tapestry spreading all across Yugoslavia. Spreading north to south, south to east, south to west... Running in all directions, subject to gradual changes, or even more often, to abrupt breaks... Suddenly the climate turns different, the landscape assumes a changed aspect.

Nature's fancy seems inexhaustible here: for in this narrow space various mountain systems converge, and the rivers flow to different seas... And it is this variety that weaves innumerable patterns into the tapestry of Nature.

Lavender plantation

Animal Kingdom

The wealth of Yugoslavia's land and sea fauna is estimated at about 30,000 species. Some of these, like eagles, bears, or the famous "man-fish", are either unknown or practically extinct elsewhere in Europe.

It is almost impossible to present a sketch survey of the wealth of *land fauna* of a country as varied as ours: it is estimated at some 23,000 species! Let us tackle it zone by zone.

The first zone, in the north-east, comprises the Pannonian plain; its southern limits are marked by the range of foothills to the south of the Sava and the Danube.

Both Yugoslav and foreign hunters praise the abundance of game and the wealth of bird population, especially waders. The most prized trophies are herons' feathers, boars' tusks and martens' furs, while the chimneys of the farmsteads are still topped by storks' nests. The greater bustard, the pelican and the capercaillie are disappearing, while the wolf, the beaver, the otter, the martin, the lynx, the wildcat and some other mammals are almost extinct. Some birds of prey, even eagles and hawks, survive in isolated hills (Fruška Gora, Papuk). There are few reptiles, and the only poisonous snakes are the adder and, on the western fringes of the zone, the horned viper (Vipera amodytes). Vojvodina is the home of the Pannonian lizard (Ablepharus pannonicus), while the brown frog (Pelobates fuscus) and the bombinator are the most important amphibians. Some endemic insects, spiders and centipedes can be found on diluvian deposits; even rarer endemic species survive on the isolated heights (Kalnik, Papuk, Fruška Gora, the hills of Banat).

The second zone, which is the largest of all, is the mountain region: it covers more than 40 per cent of the country's territory. An astonishing number of endemic species can be found here. In the Alpine section of the zone, in the extreme northwest, the white Alpine hare survives in places, while the chamois and the ibex still roam the loftiest peaks; the shaggy forests still shelter some brown bears, along with countless squirrels and doormice, while the lynx has practically disappeared (it has been reintroduced in the Kočevsko Hills, while it is still fairly frequent further south, on the Šar Planina); the wildcat has not fared much better. The white Alpine hen (Lagopus alpinus), the Alpine thrush, the Alpine wren (Accentor alpinus), the Alpine nuthatch (Tichodroma muraria), the snow jackdaw (Pyrrhocorax graculus) and the snow bunting (Calcarius nivalis) all abound in the Slovenian highlands.

In the central, or Dinaric, section of the zone a typical bird is the three-fingered wood-pecker (Picoides tridactilus), while somewhat further south the Balcanic lark (Eromophila alpestris balcanica) and the hawk (Accipiter gentilis) make their appearance, along with the mountain eagle (Aquila chrysaëtos) and several species of buzzards. The čapercaillie still nests in the most inaccessible thickets. Among the reptiles of this zone the most characteristic are the viviparous mountain lizard, the horned viper and the black snake (Tarbophis) while the amphibians are represented by several species of frogs and salamanders. Some 60 species of snails

have been recorded in the mountain regions of Bosnia, Herzegovina, Montenegro and Serbia.

The third zone stretches in a narrow belt along the Adriatic coast; it is character-

1 Family of brown bears. 2 The fox is appreciated for its fur. 3 The capercaillie is disappearing from our forests. 4 5 The ibex and the chamois inhabit the highest Alpine peaks. 6 In rutting season the woods still resound with the belling of stags. 7 The wolf is a solitary animal in summer, but bands into packs in winter. 8 The lynx survives on the Šar Planina; our snapshot is from the Kočevski Rog, where it has been reintroduced.

ized by the predominance of Mediterranean species. The prevailing mammals are small rodents, along with hares, rabbits, moles and hedgehogs. The birds include the Greek partridge, the rock dove and several gulls. There is a remarkable variety of insects, centipedes, spiders and scorpions, many of whom live beneath the stones or in rock crevices, where they are protected from heat and drought. As this region has never been subject to glaciation, numerous relic species, often of pronounced sub-tropical character, survive to the present day. The jackal finds its only European habitat on Pelješac, Korčula and Mljet; on the last-named island the imported mongoose has developed into a threat to all other animal species. No less than 22 species of bats live in this mild clime, while some of its waters (Lake Vrana, the Neretva and Bojana deltas, Lake Skadar) are veritable birds' paradises, where huge flocks assemble in the migration seasons.

On the islands (Brusnik, Vis, Jabuka, Palagruža, Sušac, etc.) some rare species and sub-species of Mediterranean lizards can be found. Another inhabitant of these islands is the Nilotic water-bug (*Belostoma nilotica*), along with the "dry stick" (*Bacillus*), exceptionally large green grasshoppers, the praying mantis and butterflies of the most grotesque shapes. A legless lizard called "blavor" (*Ophisaurus apus*) writhes its way on the ground, while Mediterranean geckos (*Hemidactylus terentola*) scale the precipitous rock walls at top speed, due to the soft pads on their fingers. Some 180 species of land snails live in the entire Adriatic zone; each island boasts its own fauna, developed in isolation. Some relict species indicate

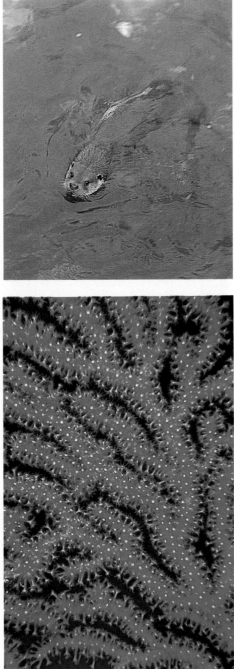

ancient land links to Italy, to Greece, even to Asia Minor, dating from the times when the Adriatic islands still formed a part of the mainland.

A second enclave of Mediterranean influence is comprised by the fauna of some sections of Macedonia, especially the Vardar valley; but here the animal population includes characteristic Aegean species, such as the Caspian turtle (*Emys caspica*), the Balcanic black scorpion (*Euscorpius balcanicus*), and even the vicious, though blind, underground termite (*Termes lucifugus*) that has become pretty ineradicable throughout the region.

The *fresh-water* fauna of Yugoslavia is no less varied: the more than 100 species of fresh-water fish assure the country one of the top places in Europe.

Most of the country's rivers belong to the Danube, or Black Sea, system. 67 species of fish inhabit this region, among them sturgeons and numerous carp species. A rare fish locally called "crnka" (*Umbra crameri*) appears in some places in Slavonia, while a species of barbel, the "lonjska mrena", is endemic to north-western Croatia.

The Vardar, or Aegean, basin contains almost 30 species of fish, among them some remarkable endemic varieties. The Drim basin, which includes Lake Ohrid, is characterized by some rare species of the carp family, like the "uklija" (*Alburnus albidus alborela*) or the "klen" (*Squalius cephalus*). Yugoslavia's southern lakes, Dojran, Prespa and Ohrid, boast each a distinct fauna of its own, due to their ages of isolation; but the most unique relic fauna is certainly that of Lake Ohrid, with its two species of trout, of which one, the endemic "belvica" (*Alburnus albidus bel-*

vica), certainly deserves pride of place; other endemic species of the lake include the "govedarka" (*Gobia gobio ohridana*), the "grunac" (*Leucos aula ohridana*), the "podust" (*Chondrostoma nasus ohridana*) and the "pijor" (*Paraphoxinus croaticus*). There are also some endemic snails whose only relatives survive in far-off Lake Baikal.

The *cave fauna* is another unique feature of the country. In the several thousand caves of the Yugoslav Karst, some 1000 species have been registered so far, and some 150,000 samples collected. The most famous representative of this underwater fauna is certainly the cave salamander called "man-fish", "olm", or *Proteus anguineus*, whose first discovery in Postojna cave caused a major zoological sensation. This pale-skinned, blind inhabitant of Karstic underground rivers somewhat resembles an elongated lizard, but wears prominent gills. Other interesting underwater inhabitants are tubeworms (*Serpulida*), originating from the Adriatic sea; the same applies to several species of blind, transparent ten-footed crustaceans (*Decapoda*).

The *fauna of the Adriatic* is also distinguished by some unique traits. The tidal zone abounds with thick-shelled snail and shellfish species capable of resisting to the surf. Various barnacles and tiny snails cling to the wet rocks of the tidal pools, while several edible varieties of shellfish, like oysters and clams, adhere to the underground cliffs. The underground "pastures" of green and brown algae and sea-weeds are the haunts of the slow-moving, delicate, blackish-brown hippocampus, curiously resembling an elaborately carved knight in a chess-set.

Further from the shore, at a somewhat greater depth, several large species of crustaceans prowl the ground: the stately lobster, and a giant crab (*Maja*) that resembles an oversized spider. Several varieties of cephalopods hide in the gloomy caves, from which their monstrous eyes lurk out for prey: the octopus and the squid, accompanied by snake-like eels, vicious congers, and sharp-toothed muraines.

Milliards and milliards of tiny plants, animals, spawn and larvae are suspended in the open sea. This plancton, freely floating with the currents, is the basic food of all other sea animals, such as the microscopic foraminifera, whose calcareous shells drop to the sea-bottom.

1 A school of salp. 2 The lobster, an inhabitant of the sea-bottom. 3 The otter is perfectly adapted to its fresh-water habitat. 4 A red coral from the Gorgonaris family.

Plant Kingdom

Due to her varied climate, pronounced relief and favourable geographical position Yugoslavia is outstanding for her wealth of flora. Three zones must be distinguished: the Mediterranean, the Continental, and the Alpine.

The species composing Yugoslavia's plant kingdom are of varied origin. Some stem from neighbouring Eastern Europe (Aralo-Caspian plants); others come from the extreme North (Arcto-Alpine species, like the birch, various rhododendrons, the edelweiss, etc.). Others again originate from the wet Atlantic districts (e. g. the ilex). A great number can be traced to various sections of the Mediterranean. But some have developed on our own soil; these are the so-called Illyrian, or Balcanic, endemic species.

Yugoslavia's flora can be divided into three distinct phytogeographical zones: the Mediterranean zone, which comprises a narrow fringe along the Adriatic coast; the Continental zone, which covers most of the country's inland regions; and the Alpine, or Nordic, zone, which includes most of the country's high mountains.

The wet grounds, which are particularly frequent in the plains region, are characterized by marshland vegetation. Along with various species of rushes and sedges, often distinguished by beautiful white and yellow blossoms, the must ubiquitous plants are water-lilies, irises and marsh-marigolds. They are found all along the river banks, especially in their backwaters, in swamps, or in the shallow stretches of rivulets, throughout the basins of the big Pannonian rivers like the Sava, the Drava and the Danube.

The faithful companions of this marshland vegetation are various riverside tree species, like the weeping willow, the white willow, the alder, the poplar, the ash.

The beauty of the meadows in the drier sections of our lowlands, e. g. of Vojvodina and Northern Serbia, is underscored by numerous Aralo-Caspian plants, some of which extend all the way to the Adriatic coast. They include various species of thistles, or the gorgeous Adonis flower (*Adonis vernalis*).

The forest cover of our continental lowlands and their hill fringe consists chiefly of various species of oak. In addition to the two common Central European oaks, the "winter oak" and the "summer oak", there are several eastern species like the "sladun" (*Quercus pubescens*) and the "cer" (*Quercus cerris*). The "summer" (peduncled, or red) oak, with its majestic trunks and kingly crowns, is the hallmark of the celebrated, once extensive, but now sadly depleted oak forests of Slavonia. The eastern varieties of oak predominate in the oak forests of Serbia, where they still cover vast areas. They also extend southwards, into Montenegro, Kosovo and Macedonia, and occasionally appear further west, in Bosnia and Croatia.

1 A splendid sight — daffodils dotting an Alpine meadow. 2 The edelweiss is the star among Alpine flowers. 3 The rhododendron — a gorgeous mountain shrub.

While the lowlands and hills of Yugoslavia are the kingdom of the oak, the mountain regions are the empire of the beech. This is the tree that gives the keynote to Yugoslavia's vast mountain forests. Of all the beech woods, the most important, from the viewpoint of exploitation, are those containing stands of spruce. They can be found all over the Dinaric range — from Slovenia, through Croatia, Bosnia and Herzegovina, to Montenegro.

Certain broad-leaved shrubs have impressed a distinctive stamp on some of Yugoslavia's mountain regions, e. g. the rhododendron, which tranforms vast stretches of the Slovenian Alps into a fabulous landscape garden, or the lilac and the cherry-laurel, which embellish whole mountain ranges in Serbia, Montenegro and Macedonia.

The spruce covers extensive highland areas of Slovenia, while the black pine and the common fir predominate in the Dinaric range, where stands of yew crown some of the highest ridges. Special attention must be given to the considerable stretches of woodland covered by endemic conifers, such as the "Pančić omorika", the "munjika", the "molika", and the Dalmatian pine.

Both from the naturalist's and from the economist's viewpoint, mountain pasturages are of prime importance. Here the number of endemic species is particularly high. They often bear the name of the region where they are encountered, e. g. the Carniolan lily (*Lilium carniolicum*), the Croatian cress (*Arabis croatica*), the Serbian pancicia (*Pancicia serbica*), the Montenegrine thyme (*Thymus montenegrinus*), etc.

Our survey of Yugoslavia's flora would be incomplete without some mention of the vegetation of our Mediterranean zone. This region features a surprising number of endemic species, and is chiefly characterized by its evergreen plants, dominated by various species of oak, like the Mediterranean evergreen oak or the Medi-

terranean black oak. The most beautiful tree of the region is, no doubt, the cypress, the symbol of the Mediterranean.

1 The svelte-crowned cypress is the symbol of the Mediterranean. 2 The mimosa — a bedizened harbinger of spring. 3 The yucca — an imported decorative plant that has struck firm roots along our coast. 4 The carline thistle decorates the meadows of our mountains and hills. 5 The Alep pine — its proud crowns surmount the Adriatic beaches. 6 Palms are the hallmark of warm climates. 7 The sunflower — another import that has struck root in our fields and gardens. 8 The fragrant cyclamen is an ornament of our woods. 9 The white water-lily is the belle of our backwaters. 10 A modest thistle may glitter like an amethyst.

Trenta Valley

*The Trenta Valley is Zlatorog's
mythic kingdom: the haunt
of chamois and eagles,
lush with medicinal herbs,
pitted with abandoned mines,
and pierced by one of the wildest
and most staggeringly beautiful
of all rivers, the Soča.*

Trenta — the name calls up the image of
the roaring Soča, the daredevil mountain
guides, the shepherds tending their flocks
on the solitary Alpine pastures, the relics
of ancient mines and ironworks; Kugy's
search for the mysterious flower called
Scabiosa trenta, and his statue looking
down on the Juliana Gardens; the fates of
Austro-Hungarian and Italian soldiers and

Russian prisoners-of-war, whose corpses
littered the valley in World War I, or the
Partisans, who resorted here during
World War II; the gaily painted roadside
shrines; and above all, the mountain
kingdom of Zlatorog, the mythic gold-
horned beast standing guard over the
craggy peaks, the passes, the abandoned
alps and forsaken mine shafts, the chamois and the eagles, the miraculous herbs
— hundreds of beckoning mysteries
fraught with thousands of perils.

As far as we know, the history of the
Trenta Valley begins with the opening of
the first mines at the turn of the 16th and

17th centuries. The valley was presumably named by the first miners, who seem to have come from the Italian town of Trento. In any case, they were soon followed by Slovenian settlers, from the Slovenian Coast, from Upper Carniola, from Carinthia, and other regions. The ore was extracted in several places on the precipitous slopes of the valley; then it was melted and forged in the ironworks set up on the river bank, opposite to the church. After a spell of prosperity the iron production started declining, and in 1778 it was definitely abandoned. Today there are hardly any traces left of this bustling activity.

After the decay of mining Trenta almost fell into oblivion, to be rediscovered, like a Sleeping Beauty, by the explorers of the Julian Alps in the second half of the last century. One day a young man called Julius Kugy turned up, itching to find the mysterious flower that the naturalist Balthazar Hacquet had described a hundred years earlier, and nobody else has rediscovered since, for it has probably never existed. But it was precisely the never-to-be found *Scabiosa trenta* that called Kugy again and again into this solitary mountain valley, and turned him into the yet unsurpassed celebrator of the Julian Alps, of Trenta's rugged inhabitants and overwhelming scenery.

As a memorial to Kugy's life-long search for the key to the mysteries of Trenta Valley, his Triestine friend Albert Bois de Chesne, in 1926, founded the "Juliana" Botanical Garden. This Alpinetum spreads on a gentle slope right under the precipitous face of Mount Kukla, not far from Trenta's little church. The garden features the entire plant population of the Julian Alps and the Karst, including, of course, all the gay flowers that dot Trenta's meadows, hill-sides and towering peaks.

Trenta's river, the Soča, rises as a wild torrent, in an inimitable shade of blue. No wonder that many eminent hydrologists consider it Europe's most beautiful river. It springs from the bottom of a huge cleft gaping in the rock face of Mount Velika Dnina. The water gushes out of a foaming cauldron, at times almost gently, at other times, such as those of spring thaws on the slopes above, with the rage of a volcanic eruption. After a hundred metres' leap it settles into a bed full of rapids, pools and boulders.

No less spectacular is the left tributary of the Soča, the Mlinarica. This torrent rises high up on the flanks of Mount Razor, then descends down a deep ravine, to stage a breath-taking show some way before its confluence with the Soča: it disappears in canyon, under thirty feet of

overhanging rocks. The canyon, protected as a natural monument, is accessible by a safe, though rather hair-raising trail.

1 Trenta is a world of its own, a preserve of unspoilt nature. 2 The Soča is a virgin beauty given to tantrums: now gently rippling, now foaming with rage. 3 5 If Trenta once attracted mystery hunters, it now casts its spell upon lovers of peace and romanticism. 4 While hunting for a mysterious flower, Kugy fell in love with Trenta, to be forever her thrall.

Postojna Cave

Through the ages the waters of the Pivka, forcing their way through the stony darkness, have sculptured a wonderland of weird shapes and dazzling colours.

Luka Čeč, a poor crofter, could not have imagined in his wildest dreams what marvellous discovery fate had in stock for him when he was told to climb a rock wall with a heavy lantern in his hand…
It all happened on 14th April 1818, when

spring was in full sway in what was then the Duchy of Carniola. Two local bosses, District Treasurer Jeršinovič and Chief Road Inspector Vidmar, were highly busy that day. For only a few days later no less a person than the Austrian emperor Franz I was to pay a visit to what was then known as the cave of Postojna; he had already seen it two years earlier, and he was so enthusiastic about it he now wanted to show it to his consort, the empress.
When the humble peasant, urged on by the two local magnates, gingerly climbed the perpendicular rock face surmounting the

river, to set up a welcome banner honouring the imperial couple, he stumbled on the entrance to another cave, an extension of the old one. But what an extension! It went on and on for miles and miles, and its breath-taking beauty was soon to eclipse all other caves of the continent.

Explorers from all over Europe rushed in; they discovered further and further extensions, dumbfounded at the ever-increasing beauty of the stalactites and stalagmites and the awe-inspiring underground canyon of the Pivka river. In the second half of the 19th century Europe's most distinguished speleologists explored here: Schmidl, Rudolf, Puttick and Martel. It was here that the first ever underground animal, a cave beetle called *Leptodirus hochenwarti*, was discovered. More and more animal discoveries followed, among them the emblem of Postojna, the world-famous cave salamander *Proteus anguineus*, the "man-skinned fish".

Postojna's cave system is, in fact, the underground course of the Pivka. The tourist itinerary mainly leads through the dry levels of the cave, from which the river has retreated to the deeper levels, where it still winds its tortuous way. The corridors abandoned by the river have since been shaped by the water trickling

in from the surface and gradually depositing the lacework of stalagmites, stalactites, pillars, curtains and other sinter formations. A diminutive electric train takes the tourists on a two-kilometre ride through the so-called Old Corridor, discovered by Luka Čeč.

In the first section of the corridor the walls look blackened. Here the Italian occupying forces kept a petrol store during World War II. On 23rd April 1944 it was blown up by a Partisan platoon. The dauntless Partisans reached the petrol containers from the unguarded opposite end of the cave, kilometres away through a maze of corridors. The resulting explosion stained the initial section of the cave. But the inner sections far outweigh this loss: the Big Mountain, where the tourists leave the train and start their walk through the cave, the Concert Hall, the

Tartarus, and the most weirdly beautiful of all, the so-called New Caves, discovered at the end of the last century. At every turn of the path, stalactites and stalagmites of the most fantastic shapes glitter in all the colours of the rainbow, reflected by the crystal-clear waters of the innumerable little lakes. The tourists hike some 5 kilometres through the maze, while the entire cave system measures no less than 16,670 metres...

Only 9 kilometres westwards from Postojna Cave is the modest village of Predjama, overhung by an imposing rock wall all riddled with holes and caves. A picturesque castle — a real eagles' eyrie — was built in the shelter of the rock in the Middle Ages. What is more, the medieval knights who resided here could defy any siege, for a natural underground passage leads to a secret exit.

The most famous owner of Predjama Castle was certainly Erasmus Luegger, a robber-knight, who lived in the second half of the 15th century and used to waylay the merchant caravans passing through Postojna. The Austrian emperor ordered the governor of Trieste, Nicholas Rauber, to lay hands on the malefactor; Erasmus entrenched himself in his castle. In vain Rauber besieged him for almost a year. Legend has it that Erasmus used to throw fresh cherries and even a roasted ox over the battlements. While the medieval castle was set deeper into the cave, its present-day successor was constructed in 1580 by the Cobenzl family.

1 2 For its wealth of stalactites Postojna Cave is unmatched in the world. 3 Proteus anguineus, the "man-fish", is the cave's most famous inhabitant. 4 Predjama Castle — an eagles' eyrie.

Mount Triglav

Yugoslavia's highest mountain is a national symbol. The Socialist Republic of Slovenia has chosen it for her emblem.

Mount Triglav, in the Julian Alps, is Yugoslavia's highest elevation (2863 metres). Nature seems to have created this majestic mountain on purpose, to give the people that settled around it and named it after a three-headed pagan god something to look up to in pride. "The Triglav is not a mountain, it is a kingdom", its passionate admirer Kugy wrote in one of his books. In his times the peak was accessible only to a handful of daring Alpinists. The first conquest of the mountain, in 1779, by a small climbing party, was one of the earliest recorded Alpinistic feats. Today the peak is accessible to just about anybody who does not mind a modicum of exertion. It is certainly the most frequented of Yugoslavia's high mountains. Here all the hikers' routes converge: the "Slovenian Alpine Trail" that crosses the Republic from end to end; the "Yugoslav Liberation Trail" that symbolizes the unity of the country's nations and ethnic groups during the Liberation War when mountains offered shelter to Tito's Partisans; and the international "Friendship Trail", which connects three countries, Slovenia, the Austrian province of Carinthia and the Italian region of Friuli.

The most remarkable feature of the mountain is, of course, its Northern Face, a sheer 2000-metre drop, one of the most staggering sights of the Alps. No other mountain face in Yugoslavia can look back upon such a rich climbing history, full of resounding triumphs and shattering tragedies. It is here that the Slovenian Alpinists pass their tests for the Himalayas and other high mountains of the world.

Another star feature of the mountain are its Seven Lakes, lined up like pearls on a string. The highest is 1999 metres above sea-level. They are fed by the melting snow, and their water ultimately disappears in the Karstic underground.

The Triglav knows only two seasons of the year. In summer it is a rendez-vous for mountaineers of all ages, nationalities and occupations. In winter it is accessible only to skilled Alpinists. So far no cable-car or other sore of civilization has been permitted to spoil the mountain, where the photographer and lover of virgin nature can still discover many a secret recess.

So the Triglav remains as it has been for ages: a proud and shapely mountain. The nation that lives on its foot has always considered it a symbol of freedom. Therefore it has adopted its three-pronged contour for its national emblem.

1 The Triglav — a symbol of freedom. 2 All the Alpine trails converge at the Aljaž Tower. 3 The mountain must be climbed, for no aerial cable-cars are allowed here. 4 The North Face — a hard test for climbers. 5 Each year in September one hundred women attempt the climb. 6 Well-marked trails crisscross the mountain. 7 The Seven Lakes are lined up like pearls on a string. Overleaf: Winter glory. Two refuges can be seen: the Planika to the left, and the Kredarica to the right of the top.

Mount Velebit

Mount Velebit is a 165-kilometre barrier skirting the sea. It separates two climates, Mediterranean and continental, and bears two contrasting faces, both rugged.

Velebit — this means, on the one hand, the virgin forests of the Lika slope; on the other hand, the strangely sculptured rocks of the Mediterranean slope.

It means the magnificent, unsullied canyons of Velika and Mala Paklenica, or the stone obelisks called Tulove Grede, rising above little pockets of flower-dotted greenery lost in the expanse of wilderness that looks like a petrified sea.

Even the western slope of Mount Velebit is not so barren as it might appear at first sight. After the rains torrents roar down the stony inclines, and in the valleys spring is in full bloom as soon as the days

become a little longer. On the Lika slope, on the other hand, the snow stays far into the spring, and the game only gradually awakens from winter torpor. The bear and the wolf are no rarity here, and nowhere else their habitat so closely approaches that of Mediterranean species, like the horned viper.

It was centuries ago that man discovered the few natural passes across the Velebit range; but the roads over the Vratnik, the Oštarije and the Mali Alan are of fairly recent date. Even later, when organized tourism set in, a few trails were laid, both across the range and lengthwise, parallel

with the sea. But outside these few paths and passes, Mount Velebit is still pretty much as Nature made it, practically undiscovered by tourists. Though its highest elevation, Vaganjski Vrh, does not exceed 1758 metres, the Velebit range remains unique and unrivalled.

From Vratnik Pass (927 metres) above Karlobag, one of the three main passages across the range, there is a breath-taking view over the blue expanse of the Adriatic, all sprinkled with white limestone cliffs.

The first writer to celebrate the Velebit range was Petar Zoranić, in his novel "Planine" (Mountains), published in 1563, one of the earliest panegyrics of high mountains in world literature.

1 The mountain range sharply divides the Mediterranean and continental sections of the country. 2 The rough stone-sculptured beauty of the Paklenica canyons. 3 The Anića Kuk is a hard nut to crack even for Alpinists. 4 Idyllic contrast: pastures surmounted by the pinnacles of Tulove Grede. 5 Sunset beyond the Kvarner Gulf.

"Devil's Town"

The towering, strange-shaped earth figures continuously created and destroyed by erosion near Kuršumlija are called "Devil's Town" by the local population.

The landscape around Kuršumlija rather resembles a game preserve or a sheep pasturage. But when you reach the highest ranges, you suddenly hit upon a most unexpected sight: row after row of towering earth pinnacles, which seem to have been set up by some crazy architect. This "Devil's Town" (Djavolja Varoš), as the local inhabitants call the natural phenomenon, covers an area of 4500 square kilometres. There is no lack of reasons for this strange appellation: for the figures of earth seem to arise by themselves, grow, disappear, reappear again, tower higher and higher, change their shapes, as if they were at the mercy of some invisible spirit that makes and unmakes them at his pleasure.

Now they resemble an array of high belfries; then, in the course of time, they are suddenly transformed into the mighty battlements of some Tartar fortress. Now again their play of lights and shadows charms up a Mediterranean town somewhere under the sun of Catalonia, or a Moorish city lost in the African deserts. Often these figures measure up to fifteen metres in height and more than four metres in width — and there are hundreds and hundreds of them. They are usually topped by stone slabs, which have resisted to wind and weather, while the surrounding ground has fallen prey to erosion.

The figures often collapse, but no less often new ones are created, and this sequence of growth and destruction has been going on for centuries.

The sight is, of course, neither an illusion nor the creation of supernatural powers, but simply a rare natural phenomenon.

Nature's strange fancy and playful whimsicality has carved these unusual shapes.

Trepča's Crystals

The gloomy pits of Trepča mine near Zvečan have yielded crystals of unsuspected shapes and colours and dazzling brilliance. Trepča's unusual "Crystals Museum" houses more than 1800 specimens — a real treasure-trove.

The underground shafts of Trepča mine near Zvečan, not far from Kosovska Mitrovica, have not only yielded rich deposits of lead ore, but also a unique collection of crystals of the most varied minerals. Both for their size, variety of shapes, wealth of colours and dazzling brilliance these specimens can hardly be matched anywhere else.

Since ancient times miners have delved for ore here. But the sweat-covered, callous-handed diggers of those times could only scratch the surface, without reaching the jewels Earth jealously hid in her entrails. It was only with the rise of industrial mining that man's dogged persistance has at long last given him access to the depths where, side by side with lead ore, the glittering crystals lay hidden. In the last few decades Trepča's miners have brought to light an unprecedented collection of Nature's artifacts. A great part of these can be seen at the Museum, which exhibits more than 1800 items. Experts have classed them into more than 50 groups. The crystals are distinguished by extraordinary splendour, vivid colours and attractive geometrical shapes, usually prisms and pyramids, whose endless combinations resemble masterpieces of modern sculpture. Every slightest change of position creates a new colour balance, a new play of light and shadows.

The largest specimens weigh a few dozen kilograms, or more. Some remind of human or animal figures, others resemble pomegranates or cragged mountain peaks. Or again, their splendour of colours reminds one of jewellery.

The Museum, which is owned by the Stari Trg mine, located in Zvečevo near Kosovska Mitrovica, also boasts some 200 crystals ceded by foreign museums, in exchange for Trepča's crystals which grace museum collections all over the world.

1 Arsenopyrite-calcite (FeAsS)-(CaCO$_3$).
2 Pyrite-flintstone (FeS$_2$)-(SiO$_2$).
3 Chalcopyrite-calcite (CuFeS$_2$)-(CaCo$_3$).
4 Calcite-plumosite (CaCO$_3$)-(Pb$_2$Sb$_2$S$_5$).
5 Flintstone-anchorite (SiO$_2$)-(Mg(Fe)CO$_3$CaCO).
6 Galenite-flintstone (PbS)-(SiO$_2$).
7 Trepča mine

Šar Planina

The mountain range is an endless succession of plateaus, where winter's mantle of snow is replaced in summer by the white flocks of sheep guarded by the local breed of shepherd-dogs, fierce fighters against the wolves.

Tetovo is situated at the foot of the extensive mountain range called Šar Planina, or simply, Šara. It is a stepping-stone towards the mountain's glorious heights. Macedonia is a country of mountains and lakes, but the Šara is her dominant range. It is both tame and savage. From November to April it is covered by a mantle of snow. Its endless grassland plateaus make it an inexaustible pasturage for flocks of sheep often counting several thousand heads. The range extends for some 80 kilometres, at a width of 12 kilometres. Its highest elevation, renamed Titov Vrh, is 2760 metres above sea-level. But its most

prominent peak is Ljuboten (2499 metres), whose characteristic shape graces the coat-of-arms of the city of Skopje.

Towering above the Polog Valley, the lush pastures of Šar Planina have fed the local flocks since immemorial times; sheep-breeding was, in fact, the economic mainstay of the region, as it was all over Western Macedonia.

In spring flowers sprinkle the green slopes, and in early summer, when the last snow-drifts have melted, the mountain is all dotted with sheep.

To escape the summer heat, the in-habitants of Polog Valley move into their snug temporary villages erected high on the hillside. In former times the Polog slopes might not have been so densely populated, but the Šara was, then as now,

the valley's main source of wealth. With one substantial difference, however: today the locals do not even need to trudge to their eagles' nests on the slopes, for a paved road leads up to them, while overhead an aerial cable-car transports tourists to the Popova Šapka.

The Šara also hides a number of lakes: Livadičko Jezero, the Black Lake, the White Lake, and many smaller ones. Both from the Titov Vrh and from the two next highest peaks, Bistrica (2640 m) and Ljubo-ten (2499), the view ranges far and wide. At the first threat of winter the flocks return to the valley, accompanied by the

world-famous local breed of shepherd-dogs, fierce and efficient defenders of flocks against prowling wolves.

1 The Šara consists of an endless succession of plateaus. 2 From spring to autumn the pastures are dotted with immense flocks of sheep. 3 The last remnants of snow, the first grass, and the first flocks. 4 The Šara is a well-equipped winter and summer resort. 5 The famous Šar Planina dogs are irreplaceable companions of the shepherds. 6 The snow reappears early in autumn, and trails and peaks remain coated in white.

Durmitor Lakes

The crystal-clear lakes of Mount Durmitor are called "mountain eyes" by the local population. According to legend, an ancient monastery reposes at the bottom of Black Lake, and winged horses ascend from Devil's Lake at night. The waters of Black Lake find their way to the Tara and the Piva by devious passages.

Jezero, is 1788 metres above sea-level. All the Durmitor lakes are clear, charming, and of easy access. They are well-frequented in summer, and ice-locked in winter.

1 The blue "mountain eyes" glitter among the peaks. Black Lake is the largest of all. 2 The mountain, with its legends, forests, lakes, snow-fields, is a world of its own, with an atmosphere of its own. 3 The scenery changes continuously, and image blends into image.

Of glacial origin, the 20-odd lakes of Mount Durmitor lie hidden in dense forest, or embedded in open grassland. They give the finishing touch to the magnificent Durmitor landscape, the craggy peaks, the shadowy woods, the high plateaus and Alpine pasturages. The description that suits them best is "mountain eyes", for their water is crystal-clear and as smooth as a mirror. It is not only their shape and their clearness that remind one of the pupil of an eye: they also reflect all the objects that surround them, the mountain tops, the dense stands of conifers, the gay petals of the mountain flowers, the white flocks of sheep on the shores, and the roe at its watering-place. According to legend, an ancient monastery lies flooded at the bottom of Black Lake (Crno Jezero), while from Devil's Lake (Vražje Jezero) winged horses soar at night, with their wings flashing like moonshine. There are also tales about most of the other lakes.

Black Lake, the largest of all, is composed of two interconnected basins, a smaller one and a larger one. The water that overflows from the larger basin at the time of the spring thaws disappears in a sinkhole near the town of Žabjak; then an underground passage leads it right beneath the Tara canyon, to reappear on the river's right bank, and join the Tara from the opposite direction. The water that drains through a sinkhole in the smaller basin, on the other hand, comes out in the Komarnica canyon, to flow into the Piva; then the Tara and the Piva converge to form the Drina. The Black Lake covers an area of 516,000 square metres, and is 1418 metres above sea-level. Its clear waters boast a visibility of 9 metres. Snake Lake (Zmijinje Jezero) is hidden in a dense forest at the height of 1495 metres, while the highest of the lakes, Malo

Marshland Bird Sanctua

Marshlands giving shelter to countless birds are important natural assets. The most famous of them are: Kopački Rit, Obedska Bara, Krapje Djol, the lower course of the Neretva, Lake Vrana, Posedarje, and the shores of Lakes Skadar, Ohrid, Prespa and Dojran.

Yugoslavia is fortunate to be one of the countries where marshlands offering favourable conditions to numerous bird species are still fairly abundant. The best-known and richest of these refuges are: Kopački Rit, Obedska Bara, Krapje Djol,

the lower course of the Neretva, Lake Vrana, Posedarje Bay, and extensive stretches of the shorelines of Lakes Skadar, Ohrid, Prespa and Dojran.

Kopački Rit, a relic of the one-time Pannonian Sea, is a vast marshland at the confluence of the Drava and the Danube, about 14 kilometres to the north of Osijek. It covers an area of 6000 hectares. In spring, when the snow begins to thaw and the rivers of the Central Danube Basin are in full spate, an average of 30,000 birds resort here. Among the dense colonies of gulls, terns, cormorants and herons rearing their nestlings in the reeds

and willows there are some bird species that are almost extinct elsewhere in Europe, such as the black stork and the white egret. Numerous species of songbirds live on the branches and in hollow trunks: finches, warblers, wood-peckers. The most remarkable bird of prey is the white-tailed eagle (*Haliaëtus albicilla*), Yugoslavia's largest eagle species.

In late autumn the waters begin to recede; together with them the huge schools of fish retreat from their native swamps, following the instinct that urges them towards the rivers. This is the time when the great autumn migrations of

birds set in. On the damp, lush-green mats of reeds, rushes and water-lilies, giant flocks of storks, herons and other waders converge, while hundreds of wild ducks dot the stretches of water. The whole landscape teems with birds feeding on the numerous fish that were too late to escape into the streams. No less than 267 bird species have been recorded in this natural preserve.

Obedska Bara, in Srem, is another marshland swarming with wildlife; unfortunately it is shrinking rapidly. The most remarkable wader living here is the sickle-bill (*Plegadis falcinellus*), whose long, thin bill curves upwards like a sickle. Another part-time inhabitant is the white stork, protected in all European countries, and the object of extensive studies of bird migrations. Storks always follow the same routes, and those of our country do not take the shortcut across the Adriatic and the Mediterranean, but follow the instinct that drives them all along the Balkans peninsula, then across Asia Minor and

Palestine to Suez, to proceed up the Nile valley to South Africa.

The comparatively small sanctuary of 25 square kilometres is visited by great numbers of birds, especially in the hot days of summer, when they feed their young. Except for the grey heron, all our species of heron nest here, such as the lesser white egret (*Egretta garzetta*), the purple heron (*Ardea purpurea*) and the yellow heron (*Ichobrychus minutus*). The white spoonbill finds its westernmost nesting places in the Yugoslav marshlands.

North-east of Zadar the Novigrad Channel, which runs along the Velebit range, extends into a bay called Posedarje; in times of migrations it is frequented by huge flocks of birds. Especially at dusk numerous exhausted migrants alight here, often after hundreds of kilometres of

uninterrupted flight across the sea. Sometimes more than 7000 birds gather in the bay at one time, from wild ducks and coots to snipes, wagtails and gulls.

Further south along the Adriatic coast, to the south-west of Biograd, is Lake Vrana (Vransko Jezero), Croatia's largest lake, with an area of 3000 hectares. It measures 13 kilometres in length, more than 2 kilometres in width, and is, in fact, a submerged Karstic valley. At its southern end the lake becomes a regular shallow swamp, covered with dense reeds and sedges. This is the favourite haunt of rails, crested grebes, wild ducks and coots. One of the finest birds is the black rail (*Fulica atra*), distinguished by a white beak and a white spot on its forehead. It dives for its prey, while its young are fit for independent life as soon as they hatch. On the wet meadows along the lake there are plenty of skylarks, pipits and lapwings — these last particularly charming with their grey plumes flapping around their heads. This is also the nesting place of Croatia's last Mediterranean colony of herons. A relative of the herons, the greater bittern (*Botaurus stellaris*), hides among the densest reeds. This cautious bird hunts only at night. The male's love song, a kind of ecstatic drumming, is heard at a distance of 3 kilometres. The brackish water hides both fresh-water and salt-water species of fish.

The lower course of the Neretva, between Opuzen and the river's delta, used to include 8 lakes, 12 backwater channels and several inlets before melioration. Of this birds' paradise only the Hutovo Blato in Herzegovina, the Prud region, Lake Kuti and the actual Neretva delta remain intact. Here great numbers of waders find a permanent habitat, while numerous birds of passage resort to these sanctuaries in the course of their spring and autumn migrations. The stagnant waters harbour a multitude of fish, especially in the spawning seasons; even some salt-water species find their way here.

The maze of canals, swamps and flooded valleys offers plenty of food and nesting space to the birds. The thick vegetation cover consists chiefly of reeds, sedges, rushes and water-lilies. The bird species include wild ducks, coots, gulls, rails, grebes, wagtails and reed-buntings, while the Hutovo Blato even houses a colony of herons.

1 In the vast marshland called Kopački Rit, at the confluence of the Drava and the Danube, up to 30.000 birds of passage find shelter in the course of their spring migrations. 2. Huge colonies of rare birds live among reeds and willows of the sanctuary. 3 Marshlands are the refuges of numerous endangered species.

Lake Ohrid

Lake Ohrid is one of the earth's oldest lakes, and its waters harbour numerous animal species long extinct elsewhere — some of them 30 million years old.

Lake Ohrid (or Ochrid) was formed long before the ice age. Wedged in between the Galičica ridge and the high mountains of the Albanian shore, it is a living relic of the earth's past.

At its »upper« end, near the monastery of St. Naum, it receives the outflow of Lake Prespa through unexplored underground passages. The lake's waters cover an area of more than 350 square kilometres, and find their outlet near the town of Struga, where the Black Drim begins its winding course towards the Adriatic.

The lake is a real museum of living fossils, a window on earth's mysteries. Its depths hide numerous animal species long extinct elsewhere — some of them 30 million years old.

The water, a fluttering emerald veil, is unmatched for its clearness: the visibility is no less than 20 metres, and the human eye can watch the gorgeous mosaic pattern of the bottom and the schools of fish crossing it. There are no less than 18 species of them. Their queen is certainly the local trout, unique for its fine taste and delicate beauty. In fact, the lake preserves two species of trout. One of them, called "letnica", descends to the depths of the lake, where it feeds on various "living fossils". Its meat is of reddish hue, and is highly prized. The second species is called "belvica", for its white meat.

On the lake bottom you may spot sponges clinging to the stones; the rushes teem with crayfish, and near the shores there

roe and expire. Their descendants once again set forth towards the haunts of their forefathers... This strange migration, covering several thousands of kilometres, was violently interrupted by the dams of the electric power stations on the Drim. Nevertheless, the lake has not been deprived of its eel population. Young eel are being brought in by tank lorries from the river's mouth, and vice versa.

In the last sunny days of autumn countless flocks of birds alight on the lake surface: grebes, ducks, geese, pelicans...

In summer the lake looks like a stretch of velvet. In winter it tends to be rough, violent and murky: storms whip up waves of 5 metres and more, just like on a sea. The lake has, however, never been known to freeze, though it is 700 metres above sea-level.

1 Lake Ohrid is not only outstanding for its beauty, but also as a veritable museum of living fossils.
2 The trout is the queen of the lake's waters.
3 The white houses of Ohrid skirt the lake.
4 Fishermen's drag-nets often reveal some relic of primeval times.

are huge schools of tiny fish called "plašica", whose scales yield the "Ohrid pearls".

Naturalists have puzzled for centuries over the mystery of Ohrid's eels. They migrate all the way from the Sargasso Sea when they are no bigger than an oleander leaf. They descend to the depths of the lake, to grow to full sexual maturity, which takes them no less than 25 years. Then, in the dusky days of autumn, they band into big schools, propelled by some primeval instinct, and make off for their native seas, where the females drop their

Djerdap Gorge

The giant dam of Djerdap Power Station, linking the Yugoslav and Rumanian banks of the Danube, has transformed the 130-kilometre gorge into a placid lake. It is the culmination of man's centuries-long efforts to subdue Europe's mightiest river.

130-kilometre Djerdap is Europe's mightiest stretch of river narrows. It is the passage cut by the Danube through the Carpathian Mountains: now a narrow canyon, now widening almost into a lake.

After the completion of the Djerdap Dam in 1971, a joint venture by Yugoslavia and Rumania, the gorge has been transformed into a placid lake, where navigation is easy. Formerly only expert pilots, well-acquainted with all the treacherous spots of the gorge, could guide the ships through it, for the river bed bristled with pointed rocks, invisible at high water. There were also dangerous whirlpools, especially in the Gospodjin Vir and Great Kazan narrows. Along some stretches the current was so wild that ships had to be tugged upstream. The Romans had al-

ready cut an artificial passage through the cliffs of the "Iron Gate", and at the turn of our century the Sip Canal was dug along the Serbian bank, where a steam locomotive used to tug the boats upstream. With the termination of the dam, all navigational worries have ceased; but the water has also flooded a number of settlements, natural curiosities and historical monuments.

In the Donji Milanovac Basin, almost midstream, there used to be an island called Poreč. After the withdrawal of the Austrian army from the right bank, in the mid-18th century, the population of the town of Banja, a few kilometres downstream, left their original settlement and founded a new one on the island, to escape Turkish reprisals. Since the island was often flooded, Prince Miloš, the first ruler of free Serbia, removed the in-

habitants to the mainland, where the town of Donji Milanovac was established, Serbia's first settlement to be built according to a development plan. It was, however, destined to move once more. In 1971 Lake Djerdap covered all its roofs; by that time the inhabitants had been resettled in a brand-new town erected two kilometres to the east.

Another picturesque island to disappear was Ada Kale, where Milenko Stojković, one of the leaders of the First Serbian Uprising, executed the ill-famed Turkish governors Aganli, Kuçukali, Mula Jusuf and Mehmedaga Fočić in 1804. Ironically, the island remained a Turkish enclave even after the victorious Second Serbian Uprising; when the islet was adjudged to Rumania, in 1913, its population was Turkish-speaking.

In the reign of the Roman emperor Tiberius, in 33 A.D., the construction of a road along the right, now Yugoslav, bank of the gorge was begun. This feat of Roman engineering was continued under the emperor Domitian, and only completed in the reign of Trajan, about 100 A.D. The road was used for pack-horse and horse-waggon trains, and for slaves tugging the boats upstream. Sections of this road, mostly hewn into the rock walls, have now been flooded by the lake. The water has also covered two stone tablets recording the construction, Tiberius's and Domitian's, while the largest and most beautiful of these tablets, Trajan's, has been removed to a new location, 30 metres higher. Downstream from Kladovo the same emperor erected a 1500-metre bridge in 133 A.D. This wonder of the time reposed on 20 pillars, each 45 metres high and 20 metres wide, and was designed by Apollodorus of Damascus.

The flooding of this extensive territory had at least one thing to its credit: it was preceded by a thorough archaeological exploration of the area, which led to a discovery of first-rate importance: the prehistoric settlement of Lepenski Vir.

1 Man has changed the wild gorge the river had cut through the Carpathian mountains into a placid lake. 2 The giant dam of Djerdap Power Station has tamed the mighty Danube. 3 The ruins of Golubac Castle guard the entrance to the gorge. 4 Trajan's tablet records the Roman engineering feats. 5 Sluices facilitate navigation through the Djerdap Dam.

Lakes Bohinj and Bled

The two mountain lakes are a mere 30 kilometres apart, but they are two entirely different worlds: one a showpiece of the primeval forces of Nature, the other of representative urbanity.

Two lakes of breath-taking beauty spread at the foot of the Julian Alps, in the very heart of Slovenia's Highland Region (Gorenjsko): lakes Bohinj and Bled.

It is difficult to explain why a lake in a setting of high mountains, such as Lake Bohinj, makes such an overwhelming impression on the beholder. Is it some primitive human urge that delights in the spectacle of water rushing downhill? Or is it rather the contrast between the placid lake surface and the wild disarray of the bleak mountain chains towering above it that forces the observer to stop short and stare? In Bohinj this contrast is a tremendous experience even today, when hotels, chalets and bungalows have mushroomed around the lake. The numerous visitors who return again and again feel each time stunned at the sight of Nature surging up to the skies, of craggy peaks outlined against the void. Further down, towards the lake, the movement gradually calms down, as the eyes pass over the rolling foothils and their wooded flanks, and then comes to a standstill as you reach the smooth lake surface. Savica Waterfall, which feeds the lake and is the source of one of the two forks of the Sava, is the spectacular climax of this natural drama — but the sound and fury suddenly dies out, and near the ancient church of St. John (Sv. Janez), where the

Sava Bohinjka flows out of the lake, the landscape is just like a peaceful epilogue, with the dramatic accents muted to an undertone.

At a time when the surroundings of the lake were even less populated than today and tourism had not made its (alas, inevitable!) impact on the region, the experience of these elementary natural contrasts must have been even more staggering. What beasts prowl in those forests beyond, the travellers would ask. What lies hidden behind that mountain range? Is there life on the snow-clad peaks? Do the ghosts of the fallen heathens still roam around the ruins of Ajdovski Gradec, where France Prešeren, in his colourful romanticist epic "The Baptism at the Savica", lets the pagan leader Črtomir make his last stand for the old religion?

Today science has supplied us with authoritative replies to all these questions, and the suspense is gone. The spell of mystery, on which the tales of suspense fed, is broken. The surrounding ridges have all been scaled, their bearings chartered, their beasts of prey exterminated; and the remains of the defenders of Ajdovski Gradec have been excavated, without anybody caring a damn about their souls… But the scenic beauty — the beauty that arises out of the clash of two contrasting natural forces — remains as awe-inspiring as ever.

Lake Bled is the exact counterweight to the primeval, elementary picturesque-

1 Picturesque, thundering Savica Waterfall: here the waters of the Seven Triglav Lakes plunge into Lake Bohinj. 2 3 The mighty ridges and the lake at their foot are inseparable. 4 The ancient church of St. John mirrored by the lake surface is a characteristic landmark of Bohinj. 5 We experience the lake as a single image; but each view is a new surprise.

ness of Bohinj. Though less than 30 kilometres of road separate the two lakes, here the high mountains form only a distant backdrop, and the lake is not set among rugged pinnacles, but embedded among gentle hummocks.

We are far from the untamed wildness of Bohinj: in Bled Nature puts on her genial, almost playful face. The ice-age glacier that chiselled it has delicately rounded of all its edges — and capriciously left a little island in its centre. The lovely island, harmoniously blending with its setting, has warmed the heart of every visitor to this region. "Ornament of heaven" is the

locals' favourite description of the island, and France Prešeren, the poet, has called Bled "the likeness of Paradise". No wonder all the peoples who successively settled the region since the dawn of prehistory have given Bled, especially its islet, a privileged place in their religious observances, underscoring its importance by appropriate buildings. Thus Bled has, from the very beginning, stood not merely for natural splendour, but rather for the exquisite harmony of architecture and landscape. The oldest of its architectural glories is the pilgrimage church on the island; slightly later is the rock-set castle;

and even younger are the numerous villas and hotels, while the village proper hides unobtrusively in the background.

The place has always attracted crowds of visitors. Europe's high society started flocking in when the Upper Carniolan Railway was constructed.

1 Lake Bled is called "ornament of heaven" by the locals, while a poet has praised it as "the likeness of Paradise". 2 For more than a century Bled has been a pioneer of elite tourism in Central Europe. 3 Rock-set Bled Castle dominates the lake. 4 The ancient boats, called "pletne", are still irreplaceable, though they must often yield right of way to regattas.

Plitvice Lakes

In a harmonious setting, 16 lakes overbrim into one another. They feature on UNESCO's list of 93 outstanding sights selected for protection by the international community.

The lakes of Plitvice form a complex hydrological system, which consists of 16 larger and several smaller lakes, arranged in a sequence of terraces, down which the water cascades in splendid waterfalls of various sizes and lengths.

Aligned in a 10-kilometre string, the lakes of Plitvice are wedged in between two mountain chains: the Liška Plješivica in the south-west, and the Mala Kapela in the north-east. The protected region of Plitvice National Park covers an area of more than 19,000 hectares, of which more than 14,000 hectares are dense forest; in some stretches the vegetation can even be described as virgin forest.

The bulk of the lake water is supplied by two rivers, the Black River (Crna Rijeka) and the White River (Bijela Rijeka), which combine into a single stream about one kilometre upstream from the first lake. Some additional water is furnished by a brook called Ljeskovac. The highest lake, Prošćansko Jezero, is 636 metres above sea-level. The remaining lakes follow in the northernly direction, connected by magnificent waterfalls, rapids, sinter curtains and ravines, gradually descending to a level 100 metres lower than that of the first lake. Finally the water tumbles down a 75-metre rock wall, to form the highest waterfall called Plitvice. The canyon at the foot of the falls is the origin of Korana river, which winds its way northwards through a succession of rock clefts.

The geological substratum of the entire Plitvice region consists of limestone and dolomite layers sedimented by the sea in the Upper Cretacean period, some 80 to 100 million years ago. The upper lakes mostly repose on impermeable dolomite strata, while the lower lakes are laid among layers of permeable and water-soluble limestone.

The lakes of Plitvice were formed and shaped by tectonic shifts, considerably abetted by water erosion, especially in the so-called ice-age; this process of transformation is silently going on today. The limestone dissolved in the water is absorbed and deposited by certain plants, chiefly algae and mosses from the genera *Cratoneuron* and *Bryum;* this results in massive sedimentation of sinter, piling up into barriers and curtains of various sizes and fantastic shapes.

The tectonic shifts, and above all, the effects of water erosion have given rise to various other karstic phenomena, like caves, sinkholes and abysses. The region counts some 36 caves.

The magnificent natural preserve is all overgrown with shaggy forest, which in some places, e.g. in the Ćorkova Uvala, bears the traits of an impenetrable primeval forest. In the eastern section stands of beech predominate, only occasionally sprinkled with yoke-elm and maple. Westwards, in the direction of the Kapela range, beech woods alternate with conifers.

Sastavci, the twin lakes that sound the final chord to the spectacle of Plitvice.

In this hospitable region several more or less endangered animal species find their natural habitat, e.g. the bear, the wolf, the wild cat, the roe deer, the wild boar, the badger, the white marten and the pine-marten. The bird population is exceptionally interesting and abundant. In the most inaccessible backwaters one can still spot an occasional otter, while the lakes and neighbouring rivers shelter some rare fish species.

1 The waters wind their unforeseeable course against the harmonious backdrop of rocks. 2 Everywhere there are falls, cascades, foaming pools, brusque changes of rhythm… 3 The creation and destruction of sinter barriers is one of the star curiosities of the lakes. 4 Winter magic: a tracery in ice.

The Drina

The once indomitable river celebrated by folk song has been turned into a string of lakes, docile, calm, but still beautiful, and greener than ever.

Foča, Goražde, Višegrad, Zvornik: these are the towns that mark the course of the Drina, a river celebrated by folk songs, expounded in voluminous books, beloved by painters.

If the river has endeared itself to singers, it has also made its name in history. Armies and generals crossed it, frontier guards and customs posts stood on its banks, travellers skirted its swift blue waters, and raftsmen navigated its rapids. Wolves howled on its banks, brigands forded it, eagles and ravens overflew it, hunters and merchants ferried across it. It meant to each what he wanted it to mean: to some it was a frontier, to others a bond of union; to some it was a canyon, a miracle of Nature, a shade of colour, a scene, to others it was just another water — the Drina!

The river had its character and its whims, it could be both good and evil. It was evil

whenever it rose and deluged its banks; in such times the ferries were hauled out of the water, and the ferrymen refused passage. The river battered against the cities on its banks, against the rock walls of its gorges, even against its own tributaries.

Then this wild, roaring river was suddenly brought to bay. A dam, put up near the town of Zvornik, has shackled its feet, and left it impotent. Where once travellers crossed by ferry, paying their tribute in silver, ducats and jewellery, the river now provides the current that lights our lamps and turns our machines.

So this water that never knew a moment's repose has been turned into a lake, docile, calm, but still beautiful, and greener than ever.

The lake varies its hue from hour to hour, just like its setting; and the setting consists now of rocks that seem to hug the skies, now of row after row of rolling green hills. The city walls of Zvornik have towered above the river for centuries. Here time seems to stand still. Illyrians, Celts, Greeks, Romans, Slavs, Turks, Bosnians — all have left their marks… The stones are stained with age. The battlements seem to be rising from the darkness of time — gazing in amazement at the miracle of miracles, the green lake spreading at their feet!

1 The Drina was once famous for its reckless raftsmen artfully navigating the dangerous rapids. 2 The green waters of the river have been harnessed by the white concrete walls of electric power-stations and transformed into a string of lakes. 3 The picturesque Drina gorges are an unforgettable experience. 4 The town of Goražde spreads on both banks.

Kravice Falls

The waters of Trebižat river suddenly fan out over an abyss, fluttering in the breeze like the mane of a prancing horse, or a flowering branch.

A rainbow, and a white curtain of water — like a fan spreading over the abyss, or a prancing white horse: these are the Kravice falls on the Trebižat river, near Ljubuški, Herzegovina.

A deafening roar, as if giants were at play here, redirecting the water, tearing out rocks, putting up their toy waterfall. A thundering noise such as only big waters can produce — you seem to be eavesdropping on the outsized harp of some ancient pagan goddess, one of those who used to protect the waters, prevent them from disappearing down some sinkhole, lest beasts of prey, cattle and birds should die of hunger, and trees and grass wither and perish.

Like a bird overflying the falls, a rainbow arches above them; as long as the sun shines, the rainbow never vanishes. But human eyes are so rare here you seem to be the first man who ever set his eye on this miracle! It resembles a painting hung on a whitewashed wall — for white rocks flank the waterfall on both sides, so it seems to be framed in by bare stone. Only here and there a poplar-tree, to make the picture stand out even sharper. The sky above, radiating the serenity of Herzegovina, makes the falls even more beautiful, their water even clearer, their foam even whiter. At night, under the bright starlight, the waters glitter as if molten silver was cascading down the rocks — with all the ring, the shivery clink of real silver...

The Kravice Falls resemble the mane of a galloping horse, or a flowering branch fluttering in the wind. They seem to have been created on purpose — as a show-piece of Nature, to prove to mankind what amazing tricks she can play with water. All for our own benefit — so we can come and watch her at her play, clad in sunshine and all the hues of the rainbow. And when we leave, we seem to have dreamt it all.

Here, on the Trebižat river, in the heart of stony Herzegovina, the Kravice Falls form a filigree pattern.

Lake Skadar

This largest lake of the Balkans covers, depending on the season, an area of 370 to 540 square kilometres. Its shores shelter some rare plants and birds, while its waters contain 35 species of fish. On some of the 50-odd islands there are ancient monasteries and castles.

Lake Skadar can be negotiated in two directions. Either east to west, setting out from Krajina; this was the direction in which the political and ecclesiastical centre of the region shifted through the centuries: Skadar – Krajina – Vranjina – Žabljak – Obod – Cetinje. Or west to east, embarking at Rijeka Crnojevića, beneath the ruins of Obod. The advan-

tage of starting from this point is in the unforgettable view of Rijeka Fiord and Lake Skadar you can glimpse from the road as you approach Rijeka Crnojevića. It is a scene dozens and dozens of painters have tried to capture on their canvases – there must have been more of them than could fill a large gallery.

Lake Skadar has been associated with books since ancient times. Monks compiled and copied medieval manuscripts in the monasteries perching on the lake's islets. In 1494 the first printing house among the Southern Slavs was set up in the fortress of Obod. Today the lake itself

is the object of voluminous scientific treatises.

For Lake Skadar — at one time a branch of the sea — is not only a first-rate natural phenomenon in itself, but also remarkable for its historical sights. Owing to its easy accessibility, mild climate and fertile hinterland, it has always played a distinguished part in history.

If one attempted to record all the wars waged around the lake and trace all the civilizations that left their stamp on its shores, one could compile a bulky folio: Illyrians, Goths, Avars, **Tartars, Greeks,** Romans, Slavs, Turks would all play star roles in it... Today there is hardly a country in the world that does not send tourists, sports fishermen or researchers here — and not one of them returns empty-handed, disappointed or indifferent to the experience.

Lake Skadar is the largest lake of the Balkans. Depending on the water level, it covers an area of 370 to 540 square kilometres, while its depth is no more than 1 to 44 metres. Its surface is, depending on the season, some 12 to 15 metres above sea-level, while its deepest spots reach below sea-level (a phenomenon scientists call "cryptodepression"). In addition to being Yugoslavia's largest sweetwater fishing ground, it is one of Europe's major bird sanctuaries. It is dotted by no

less than 50 islands. Its shores shelter some rare plants and birds, while its waters contain 35 species of fish.

Some of the islands boast important historical and cultural monuments, from monasteries to fortresses. On the island of Vranjina a monastery was erected in the 13th century; it was the episcopal see of the first bishop of Zeta. Another monastery, on the island of Baška, is a foundation of Jelena Balšić from the 15th century. The islet of Starčevo holds the tomb of the famous printer Božidar Vuković, who died in 1540, after he had been awarded the title of "Duke of Printing". On the island of Kom the great poet and statesman Njegoš was ordained an archimandrite. Another island, Žabljak, served as the first capital of the Crnojević dynasty, while the islets of Lesendar and Grmožur sport ancient Turkish fortresses and casemates. Laurel-trees spread their blossoms on Mala Gorica and several other islands.

1 Lake Skadar is a lake with a difference: both its scenery, its beauty, its history, its birds, its fish and its floating water-nuts set it apart from all other lakes. 2 Rijeka Crnojevića has been a fishing village since immemorial times. 3 A quiver spreading across the lake surface.

Adriatic Fiords

The Adriatic coast is not only fringed by a thousand islands, but also indented by a succession of bays and inlets, of which some are real fiords, cutting deep into the rugged mainland.

Some 5 kilometres to the north of Rovinj and 10 kilometres to the south of Vrsar, the Lim Channel notches the Istrian peninsula: about 9 kilometres in length, and an average 600 metres in width. Sailing up the inlet you notice, after a mile, the entrance to a cave among the cliffs of the northern shore. This is the famous grotto of St. Romuald, who came into the region in the 11th century, established a monastery on the Lim Channel, and at last retired to the solitude of this cave.

The inlet has always abounded in fish: as early as 534 A.D. it is mentioned as a fishing-ground in a deed of cession that bears the signature of bishop Euphrasius, more famous as the founder of mosaic-studded Poreč Basilica. The inmost section of the channel has been converted into an oyster and clam farm.

An entirely different type of fiord is found at the mouth of the Krka. There the spacious Šibenik Channel leads through a bottleneck passage called St. Anthony's Channel, among a maze of little islands, into the wide Šibenik Basin, on whose north-eastern shore the ancient city of

Šibenik rises amphitheatrically above its busy port.

Perhaps the closest replica of a Scandinavian fiord is the channel formed by the submerged course of the Zrmanja river. Its one-time mouth, the Novsko Ždrilo strait, is a tortuous passage between rock walls. Further upstream the channel widens into the ample Novigrad Basin; it is precisely at this point that the Adriatic Trunk Road crosses on an elegant bridge. The Zrmanja reaches the Novigrad Basin through a deep canyon cut into solid rock; but even here the water is not fresh, but salty, so the gorge is, after all, a fiord. The view is particularly impressive from the plateau flanking it. What distinguishes the channel from a Norwegian fiord is the hue of its waters, not dark green, but emerald blue. The inlet can be navigated up to Obrovac, and even further; all the time the view is arrested in the north by the rock face of the Velebit range.

But it is in the Boka Kotorska that the sea pierces deepest into the continent. This odd-shaped fiord consists of three basins. The outer basin is called the Gulf of Hercegnovi, the central one the Gulf of Tivat, and the inmost recess, the Gulf of Kotor. The entrance to the Boka is guarded by Mamula island. Along the northern shore of the Gulf of Hercegnovi the settlements form a continuous string. The westernmost outpost, at the mouth of the Sutorina, is Igalo, a well-known spa, whose radioactive waters are indicated for rheumatic complaints. Slightly further east is the town founded in the 14th century by the Bosnian king Tvrtko as Sveti Stefan; it achieved its highest bloom in the reign of Duke ("herceg") Stjepan Vukčić Kosač, after whom it was given its present appellation of Hercegnovi.

Even further eastwards, along the northern fringe of the Gulf of Tivat, is a cluster of ancient towns: Zelenika, Kumbor, Djenovići, Baošići, Bijela and Kamenari. On the eastern shore there is the city of Tivat, and to the south of it, a little island once called Stradioti, after the Venetian mercenaries who garrisoned it, and today renamed Sveti Marko and converted into a holiday resort.

The Gulf of Tivat is separated by the Verige Strait from the Gulf of Kotor. On its western shore we pass Stoliv, Prčanj and Muo, and at the southernmost extremity of the fiord, almost 39 kilometres from the open sea, we reach the city of Kotor.

1 Zavratnica — a little cove carved in solid stone.
2 The Lim Channel cuts deep into the Istrian peninsula, half-way between Poreč and Rovinj.
3 The most impressive and colourful of the Adriatic fiords is the Boka Kotorska.

Susak

This in an island of sand — an exception among Adriatic islands. Everything is different here: the scenery, the population, the dialect, the costumes, the traditions.

Susak is the only Adriatic island made of sand — four square kilometres of nothing but sand. Reposing on a limestone base, it towers in up to 100-metre-high sand hills, all covered by reeds and vineyards.

The local women wear light slippers of kid leather, curiously resembling ballet slippers. On any of the stony islands such footwear would hardly last from dusk to dawn… But there are no stones here. Even building stone must be shipped in from the neighbouring islands… Vegetation is scarce, however, for nothing but reed and vine will grow here; but the latter seems to thrive exceptionally well on sandy ground, therefore the wines of Susak are outstanding, though they do not travel well.

The islanders seem to be pretty self-sufficient. For centuries they were left to their own resources, and in their struggle with cruel reality there were only two courses open to them: to hold on, or to emigrate. They have, understandably, always enjoyed the reputation of good sailors, especially pilots. A street in Hobboken in the state of New York, U.S.A., is a kind of second Susak: it is inhabited by ten times as many islanders as the island itself. For there are only 280 people left among the native sands and vineyards, while Hobboken holds no less than 2800 of them! But a great number of them return when they reach the age of retirement. The ancient graveyard is situated on the highest elevation of the island. The tombstones do not bear more than ten surnames, of which only four reappear with

any frequency. They all belong to families immigrated, according to tradition, from Crimea on the Black Sea. The most ubiquitous surname is Tarabochia. This is supposed to be the Italianized version of the Turko-Tartar name "Karabok" or "Kara-bogh", which means "invalid". The descendants, however, seem to enjoy perfect health and reach a high àge.

Whoever wished to stick it out on the island, had to fall back on the sea and the vineyards. These have moulded a special cast of people. The women are distinguished by high, prominent foreheads, hazel eyes, and locks of raven hair spilling from their supposedly black scarves bleached by the salty breezes. The islanders speak a peculiar blend of Serbo-Croatian and Italian, which is not understood even on the neighbouring island of Lošinj.

The folk costumes, too, are vastly different from the "classical" costume worn all along the Adriatic coast. Instead of the usual long skirts, the local beauties wear a kind of bell-shaped mini-skirt, allowing a glimpse of the starched and lace-lined petticoat beneath.

1 2 The island is a quirk among Adriatic islands: a hundred metres' layer of sand reposing on a limestone base. 3 The women's costume is a kind of mini-skirt. 4 Women can be still seen balancing burdens on their heads. 5 The island's peaceful harbour.

Kornati Islands

The archipelago lies deserted today, but it can look back on a long, though half-forgotten history. The lush green groves have been destroyed by a fire that raged for 40 days and left only bare rocks behind.

According to ancient land registers, the Kornati Islands consist of 8 major islands, 109 islets and 30 cliffs. It is the most numerous archipelago of the Adriatic. There are no permanent settlements now on any of the islands. The inhabitants of the neighbouring islands come here periodically to till their fields, tend their sheep or catch fish. In the coves of the islands some 250 stone houses offer shelter from the winds.

The archipelago is called after the largest island, Kornat. It is already recorded in the oldest Venetian maps, for it was a hazard to navigation. The oldest name for the island is recorded in 950 A.D. by Constantine Porphyrogenetus as "Grebeno". The present name is derived from the Italian word "corona", crown. Indeed, the islands do look like a crown of white stones.

The archipelago is deserted today, almost uncanny in its solitude. At one time it was covered by dense woods. In the mid-19th century the Kornati Islands were ravaged by a fire, which raged for 40 days. The wind carried the fiery sparks from island to island, and from the mainland it looked as if the sea was on fire. Since then the vegetation has not been able to recover. The seas around the archipelago abound in fish, especially lobsters and other crustaceans. In every cove where seasonal fishing settlements have been erected, the sea bottom is all covered with large osier baskets of unusual shapes. They taper off towards the open bottom, where a bait is placed. The lobster squeezes into the trap, but cannot escape through the bottleneck…

This wasteland, lost between the blue of the sky and that of the sea, looks as god-forsaken as if it had never harboured any life. Nevertheless, the Kornati Islands can look back on a history of their own, reaching down to the Neolithic age. Apparently, Neolithic man, whose stone adze has been unearthed on Piškera island, must have been provided with rafts or boats. In Piškera Strait the walls of a Roman tollhouse still resist to the times. In the Middle Ages the islands were a refuge for numerous fugitives from the mainland.

Life has changed since. In ancient times, when fishermen used only rowing and sailing craft, they were forced to stay on the Kornati Islands for much longer periods than nowadays; therefore the archipelago seemed to teem with life.

1 The Kornati Islands look almost unearthly: a handful of ducats lost in the blue of the sea. 2 Though the archipelago is uninhabited today, its vast schools of fish attract fishermen, adventurous yachtsmen and would-be Robinsons.

Mljet

Here everything looks different: the blue tracery of the stone-laced inlets, or the two lakes — one graced by an island monastery...

Mljet — the name evokes the fragrance of Alep pines, myrtle and wormwood; the blue tracery of the stone-laced inlets.

More than two thirds of the island are covered by lush pine forests, oak groves and evergreen shrubbery. Because of its exquisite beauty and luxuriant vegetation a large part of the island is protected as a national park. This latter includes the two splendid lakes — the Great Lake and the Little Lake — connected to the sea by a narrow channel. In the centre of the larger lake is an island with an ancient Benedictine monastery.

The island's main village, Veliko Polje, is also called Babino Polje ("Old Hag's Field"), for according to tradition the place was at one time ruled by an old

woman. This folk legend is often considered to refer to the nymph Calypso, whom Greek mythology placed in a cave on the island of Ogygia, commonly identified with Mljet. The grotto still exists, and is now called Galičnjak. Here, if credit can be given to the tale, Odysseus spent seven years of his wanderings in the embrace of the perfidious nymph.

Much later the Roman emperor Septimus Severus exiled on the island — then called Melitta — the patrician and poet Agensilaus. The banished poet wrote to the emperor: "In this place where birds sing on the green pine branches and the seas

The past is ever-present. In Polače, for instance, the remains of one of the oldest Roman monuments on the Adriatic decay among the vineyards and olive groves. Those Romans certainly knew how to choose their pleasure resorts! For the ruins are the relics of a Late Hellenistic patrician villa, complete with fortifications. Tradition records it was here that the Cilician poet Oppianus wrote his poems on fishery and bird-hunting.

When night stealthily descends on the woods of Mljet, all things suddenly seem to commune with one another and fuse with one another under the star-lit summer sky. Day surrenders to night, the ancient walls to the pine-trees, the immortelle to the rosemary, the fragrance to the sea breezes, the white of the sands to the blue of the sea, the islands to the immense sky that engulfs them.

1 3 You cannot help returning to Mljet again and again — both for its splendid lakes and its exceptional atmosphere of peace. 2 Melitta — an inspiration for poets.

play with the beaches of the rounded coves, there is no room for evil or sadness..."

The poet lived on the shores of the Great Lake (Veliko Jezero), where Benedictine monks erected an island monastery in the 11th century, today adapted as a hotel. It is flanked by the Romanesque church consecrated to "Our Lady of the Lake". There are no more Benedictines on the island, except those reposing under their limestone vaults. Behind the ancient walls camphor-trees spread their flowering boughs, and when their fruits ripen, they drop on the stone slabs like a hermit's tears.

Footprints of Time

Years are of no consequence, though they are counted in hundreds and thousands. For man's footprints leave marks not even time can erase. That is why there are so many indelible records of man's passage through the ages: the sandstones of Lepenski Vir, the mosaics of classic antiquity, the medieval graveyards of stećaks, mighty ruins of castles and fortresses, or humble roadside tombstones…

Mosaic from Heraclea

Krapina's Primitive Man

The cave of Hušnjakovo Brdo near Krapina is a treasure-trove of relics of ancient man. It is one of the most authentic records of man's early development.

In 1899 – 1905 the Zagreb paleontologist Dragutin Gorjanović-Kramberger exca-

vated one of the richest and most important sites of fossil man at Krapina in the Croatian Zagorje region.

The sand strata of an open cave on the slope of Hušnjakovo Brdo Hill yielded about 650 fragments of bones or skeletons of primitive human beings of both sexes; their age ranges between 2 and 40. Along with these remains of at least 20

individuals (or 60, according to a detailed analysis of their teeth), a great number of stone and bone implements have been found, such as scrapers, borers, awls, cutters — real masterpieces of primitive craft. A wedge-shaped bone splinter, some 12 centimetres in length and probably stemming from the tibia of a rhinoceros, apparently served as an adze. A small, half-carbonated chip of beech-wood shows that these people used fire; this is also confirmed by several singed bones, by traces of ashes, and above all, by the stone-lined primitive fireplaces.

Among the few thousand fragments of teeth and fossilized bones of various animals contemporary with the Krapina Man, more than 700 bones of the cave bear have been unearthed. There were also well-preserved remains of the rhinoceros, the aurochs, the grizzly bear, the primitive horse, the wild boar, the mammoth, three species of deer, the wolf, the beaver, the marmot, the hamster and the rat — in total, 18 species of mammals, in addition to 3 species of birds and 1 species of tortoise.

Judging by their physique, their way of life and their material culture, the Krapina People resorted to the cave several times through a long period. This is proved by the fact that the successive strata show not merely varying fossil remains of men and animals, but also different cultural horizons, each with its typical tools, artifacts and fireplaces. The bottom of the cave was apparently levelled and re-settled at intervals.

In those times a fairly large and deep river, the ancestor of the present-day Krapinica, passed at the mouth of the cave. Today the river-bed is eroded, and the water-level is 25 metres lower than in those days. Due to constant erosion and landslides, the cave was wholly filled up with sand before the excavation, which had to remove an 8-metre layer of dirt. The site is considered to be at least 30,000 to 60,000 years old.

The average height of the Krapina Man was about 160 centimetres; his body was slightly bent, and his skull distinguished by a low, slanting forehead, prominent eyebrows, and a rather slender chin. All these are characteristics of the Neander-tal type. But there seem to have been two racial varieties: one strong and robust, and the other gracile and delicate. Both lived during the last period of glaciation, probably in intervals with a comparatively mild climate. Canibalism cannot be excluded: it might be implied from the numerous remains of carbonated, singed and split human bones. There is, of course, the intriguing possibility that this ancient and primitve type of man was victimized by the stronger, more intelligent and more efficient ancestor of modern man, Homo sapiens fossilis.

The fossil remains of Krapina are today exhibited in Zagreb's Geological and Paleontological Museum. Around the Krapina cave itself, lifelike models of cavemen have been set up, arranged in groups that portray their way of life.

1 An ambush on Hušnjakovo Brdo Hill: primitive man in one of his aggressive postures. 2 A primitive fireplace: fire was the mainstay of Krapina's ancient man. (Reconstructions)

Lepenski Vir

Lepenski vir is a testimony of man's earliest artistic creativity, of functional houses and representative sandstone statues — precious links bridging the abyss of time.

So far it had been generally assumed that at the dawn of civilization Europe was no more than a cultural dependency of the Middle East. Lepenski Vir is an eloquent testimony to the contrary.

Lepenski Vir is, in fact, the name of a big river whirlpool and its basin, mid-way down the Djerdap Gorge. This was the birthplace of one of Europe's earliest cultures, bridging three ages of human prehistory (paleolithic, mesolithic, neolithic). The excavations were carried out between 1965 and 1970. A three-and-a-half metre productive layer has yielded the remains of nine successive building horizons, dividing the culture into five basic periods.

The absolute chronology of this culture cannot be verified by the classical "historic" method. But the findings can be dated by radiactive carbon isotope measurements, as well as by geological, paleontological and anthropological comparisons. All these methods agree that man lived in the locality as early as the turn of the 8th and 7th millenniums B.C., while in the 6th millennium B.C. Lepenski Vir was a flourishing fishermen's settlement and major religious and cultural centre.

Of the oldest settlement of the pre-neolithic period, so-called "Pre-Lepenski Vir", only meagre traces have been preserved: fireplaces and domestic utensils of bone and stone. A younger settlement, "Lepenski Vir I", consists of a compact cluster of houses, whose shapes and arrangements remain unchanged throughout the five building horizons. The youngest of the pre-neolithic settlements, "Lepenski Vir II", was constructed on the ruins of its predecessor; its houses were, in their turn, largely destroyed when "Lepenski Vir IIIa", an outpost of the neolithic Starčevo Culture, was established in its place.

The characteristic architecture of trapezoid houses fascinates by its beauty and its spatial arrangement, which allows free movement along the two main traffic arteries, bearing evidence of the architects' sense of functionality.

The architecture is matched by the sculpture. The monumental sandstone figures were firmly planted around the fireplaces; they served as guardians of the place until the Lepenski Vir culture was extinguished.

The creators of the Lepenski Vir culture of pre-neolithic periods belonged to a strong and robust Europoid type. The inhabitants of the neolithic settlements are of more delicate build and belong to the Mediterranean type, whose culture was no more based on hunting and fishing, but on livestock-breeding and agriculture. The representatives of the Starčevo Culture only lived in Lepenski Vir as long as the poor soil of Djerdap Gorge allowed them: there is not much arable land in this mountain-ringed basin. Therefore they had to move, even before the close of the Lower Neolithic, to the plains east and west of the Gorge.

1 The archaeological discoveries at Lepenski Vir have radically altered our knowledge of man's early creative achievements. 2 3 The purposeful architectural solutions are matched by the strange-shaped figural sculptures in sandstone.

Daorson

The cyclopean walls rising on the Ošanići heights above Stolac once held the capital city of the Illyrian Daorsi tribe, and recall ancient Mycenae. Prosperous Daorson, which coined its own money, went up in flames after a fight with the neighbouring Dalmati tribe.

The Ošanići rise above the town of Stolac, Herzegovina, and the Daorsi were an Illyrian tribe that lived here since

pots. Smoke arose from their hearths — until one day the fire went out forever, and the city died out. Only the oversized stones remain, to remind us that the world was not created by our generation. It must have been a rich town indeed, for it coined its own money. Its flocks must have grazed on the mountain pastures rising to the north and the east; the fertile Radimlja plain to the south must have been the city's bread-basket. There was only one hitch: the wheat grew deep down in the valley, and it must have been

the dawn of history, establishing a city named Daorson by the Greeks.

The Daorsi traded with the Greek colonies on the coast, selling their cattle, milk pruducts, wax, honey and meat, and buying spears, arrows, armours, textiles, silks and salt in return.

Daorson looms on its rock summit, among the clouds, a real eagle's nest. Its life stopped still some 2000 years ago, while the walls remain, recalling ancient Mycenae. In fact, this is a second Mycenae: the same cyclopean walls and the same huge stone blocks were used in both places.

The sherds of earthenware pots, jars, bowls — these are, along with the walls, the only traces of human occupation left in the once mighty fortress of Daorson. There was a time when people drank water from these jars and cooked in these

a back-breaking job to haul the harvests uphill to the city. And to make it even worse: there was no running water in Daorson, so it had to be brought from far away. But once their labours were done, the citizens could eat and drink safely behind their walls: there was no fear anybody could chase them from their banquet-tables sagging with bread and wine. For Daorson was considered impregnable: a system of towering walls built on solid rock, high up in the skies. Yet, in the mid-1st century A.D. the city went up in flames, after a fight with the neighbouring Dalmati tribe, with whom Daorson had been at loggerheads for over a century.

1 The ruins of Illyrian Daorson are still impressive, though ravaged by the tooth of time for some twenty centuries. 2 The city perches high on a hill, with the Vidoško Polje spreading below.

Stobi and Heraclea

Livy, the Roman historian, mentions Stobi as an "ancient city", while Heraclea was founded in the 4th century B.C. by Philip II of Macedonia. The remains of both cities witness their high level of civilization.

In the first millennium B.C. the middle course of the Vardar was settled by the Paeonian tribes. In Roman times one of their main centres, Stobi, grew into the largest city of northern Macedonia. Its location at the confluence of two rivers, Axios and Erigon, is symbolically represented on a Roman coin showing an Amazon flanked by two nymphs.

Archaeological findings prove that Stobi was established in the Greek period. Livy, the Roman historian (59 – 17 B.C.), already calls it an "ancient city". In the reign of Augustus it became a Roman "oppidum"; somewhat later it was granted municipal rights, and the local mint coined its own money inscribed "Municipium of Stobi". In the 1st century A.D. the

city expanded. Luxurious private houses were erected, decorated by frescos, reliefs and mosaics. At the turn of the 2nd and 3rd centuries a monumental theatre arose near the forum; its architectural features are Greek rather than Roman. Greyish-white marble from the nearby Pletvar quarries was used in the construction. Beneath the scene there was a temple of the goddess Nemesis, the personi-

1 Stobi is a dead city, but archaeologists have patiently and painstakingly excavated and reconstructed this hypocaust, which served to heat the public baths. 2 Heraclea was a city of magnificent buildings. 3 Mosaics of Stobi.

fication of conscience, honour and justice. After the close of the 3rd century the theatre was chiefly used for gladiatorial games. The torso of an unidentified Roman emperor has been found among the ruins. The main city gate, Porta Heraclea, is contemporary with the theatre.

The private houses of the imperial period were furnished with numerous statues of marble or bronze, consecrated to various deities like Aphrodite, Serapis, Pan, nymphs and satyrs. Among the numerous palaces bespeaking the prosperity of the city the most magnificent belonged to a certain Parthenios.

At the end of the 4th century the first Christian churches were constructed. Stobi soon became a bishop's see. Several basilicas stand on the foundations of earlier buildings. Thus bishop Philip erect-

ed a large cathedral right over the abandoned amphitheatre, no doubt as a symbol of the victory of the new religion. In the late 5th century Stobi was ravaged by the Gothic king Theodoric the Great. In the following century the city was devastated by an earthquake. Barbarian incursions from the north gave it the finishing-stroke.

Stobi is not the only ancient city unearthed in the region. In southern Pelagonia the Hellenized Macedonian ruler Philip II, who claimed his descent from Heracles, founded the city of Heraclea in the 4th century B.C. It was intended as a stronghold on the frontier between the Macedonian kingdom and the free Illyrian tribes, on the Via Egnatia, the main traffic artery and commercial route linking the Adriatic and the Aegean.

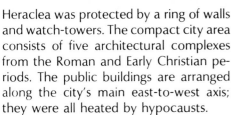

Heraclea was protected by a ring of walls and watch-towers. The compact city area consists of five architectural complexes from the Roman and Early Christian periods. The public buildings are arranged along the city's main east-to-west axis; they were all heated by hypocausts.

Among the numerous works of sculpture excavated in Heraclea, the most remarkable is a statue of Athene Parthenos − a Roman copy in white marble of the celebrated masterpiece by Phidias.

The Roman period is represented by several monumental buildings. The amphitheatre, dating from the reign of Trajan, was not only used for theatrical performances, but also to stage gladiatorial fights; a high partition was erected around the orchestra to protect the public from the furious beasts.

In the Early Christian period, from the 4th to the beginning of the 5th century, Heraclea was an episcopal see, whose occupants took part in the synods of Serdica, Ephesus and Constantinople. Several splendid churches were constructed in the 5th century; they excel by their monumental design, their wealth of colour, and the complicated symbolism of ornaments. At the close of the century the city was laid waste by Theodoric. It revived in the early 6th century, to enjoy a new lease of peace, until it was definitely abandoned after the arrival of the Slavs.

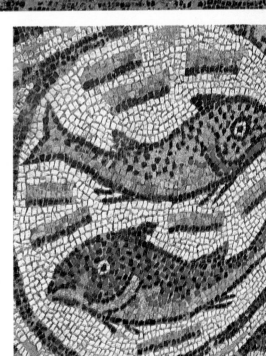

1 Several precious statues have been unearthed among the walls of Heraclea. 2 The amphitheatre of Stobi was not only intended for theatrical performances, but also served to stage gladiatorial fights. 3 4 5 The mosaics of Heraclea, outstanding for their exuberance of colour, motifs and composition.

Diocletian's Palace

At the foot of Marjan Hill emperor Diocletian built a vast palace — a cross between a luxurious villa, Roman military camp and Hellenic city. This

core of the modern city of Split is UNESCO-protected as a part of the world's artistic heritage.

At the foot of Marjan Hill the Roman emperor Diocletian, who ruled from 284 to 305 A.D., constructed a vast palace, where he spent the last days of his life in peaceful retirement.

The Dalmatian-born emperor had risen from the ranks. After his soldiers had appointed him emperor, he spent most of his life campaigning on various frontiers of his empire. Weary of his authority, he at last decided to retire. He had a palace constructed on the site of the ancient settlement of Aspalathos, not far from Salona, the capital of Roman Dalmatia. The building faced a quiet, sunny gulf, protected by a ring of islands; what is more, it was located in the vicinity of sulphureous springs, for the emperor was plagued by that eternal affliction of sol-

diers — rheumatism. The natural beauties of the site were coupled with considerations of safety: the ex-emperor probably felt best defended here, among his crack Illyrian legions.

The unique, overwhelming construction still stands today, after almost seventeen centuries of occupancy, with its outside walls hardly altered at all — the only exception being the sea-front. The palace was originally built on the very shore, so the emperor could embark straight from the Sea Gate; since the Middle Ages Split's celebrated seaside promenade, the "Riva", has been laid out between the palace and the sea.

Architects from both East and West took part in the construction; this is reflected in the blend of stylistic elements. Indeed, the palace has been described as a "cross between a luxurious villa, Roman military camp and Hellenic city". Its ground-plan forms a huge rectangle; sixteen towers, most of them pulled down since, served to protect the building. Only two of the towers surmounted the sea-front; from their height the Roman guards could survey the movements of galleys in the bay, or dreamily watch the sunshine reflected from the ripples, and the white foam raised by the southern winds.

In the Vestibule, the entrance hall to the emperor's private appartments, the Split

Summer Festival is held now, while various other halls serve for congresses. The centre of the palace, on the crossroads of the two main thoroughfares linking the Golden, Silver, Iron and Sea Gates, is the Peristyle, a giant colonnade leading up to the emperor's mausoleum, since transformed into St. Duje's Cathedral. At the entrance two sphinxes resist the tooth of time, looking down on the bustle of strollers hurrying towards Split's popular

main square, the Narodni Trg, where the ancient Gothic town hall today serves as an Ethnographic Museum.

1 Diocletian's palace is one the monuments created only once in an age: bird's-eye view of the Peristyle. 2 One of the Peristyle sphinxes. 3 View of the southern façade. 4 The Peristyle is the heart of the palace: entrance to St. Duje's Cathedral. 5 Split's famous "Riva" was built against the southern façade of Diocletian's palace.

Stećaks

The medieval tombstones of Bosnia and Herzegovina are the most original aspect of Yugoslavia's rich cultural heritage. The white marble slabs, still defiantly upright, are eloquent testimonies of bygone times.

The stećaks, or medieval tombstones of Bosnia and Herzegovina, have been called the most curious necropoles on earth; even sober scholars have to admit there is nothing that even remotely resembles them.

They are enormous blocks of stone, usually distinguished by an inscription beginning with the words: "Ase leži...", which means: "Here reposes..."

They are scattered throughout Bosnia and Herzegovina — anywhere people used to live and die. But their times are gone for good. For they belong to the period of the Bosnian rulers Tvrtko, Dabiša and Ostoja; of Stjepan, duke of Herzegovina, and Miroslav, prince of Hum.

One of these marble slabs reads: "Here I stopped, praying to God and not thinking any evil; but lo, thunder struck me!" This short message, penned some time in the reign of Dabiša and Ostoja, does not strike us as sad; rather, it seems to convey a protest against death.

There are innumerable such messages: tens of thousands of stećaks have been registered. Their inscriptions constitute a real ancient literature in stone.

There are monumental stećaks: some measure up to 2 metres in height. Their texts are often gay, even jocular; only occasionally tinged by sadness.

In their strange way, they carry on a conversation about the vagaries of human destinies. One of them, for instance, puts it: "Here reposes Ozrislav Kopijević. I have been pierced, I have been slashed, I have been skinned, but I have not died of it. I just closed my eyes on the day of Christ's Nativity, and my lord, the duke, buried me and set up this memorial." Another is even more lapidary: "When I most wanted to live, I died." The tombstone commemorating a certain Dipac the Goldsmith reads like a confession: "Whomever I served in life, I served faithfully."

"My family, regret me!" is the outcry of Bokčin, son of prince Stipko Ugrinović from Kotorac. "Young I left this world, my mother's only son."

Another man, whose name is not recorded on the stone, puts it even more succinctly: "I was born to great rejoicing, I died to deep mourning."

"I beseech my brothers and my lords to let my bones repose in peace," a certain Pavko chiselled on his block of marble. Needless to say, his tombstone has crumbled to pieces, and his mortal remains have been spread to the four winds.

"While I existed, I was honest and gallant!" duke Radivoje Oprašić proudly records on his slab.

A man called Grahovčić, from the village of Brajkovići, emphasizes his book-learning, defining himself as "a man who thought rightly, prayed to God and knew his Book by rote."

There are no dates, of course: not a single one of these tombstones can be precisely dated, except occasionally by the reign of some obscure Bosnian prince. The script is cyrillic; but it differs considerably from the cyrillic used by the church, and the characters have, to all appearance, been often chiselled by an unpracticed hand. But the thought expressed on the stone is never naive or vulgar: it always expresses a striking, observation on life — poetical rather than religious.

1 Radimlja, near Stolac, is one of the most representative necropoles, containing stećaks of all shapes. 2 This stećak from Zgošća, near Kakanj, is the most elaborately sculptured of all; it has been transferred to Sarajevo's Provincial Museum. 3 Graveyards of stećaks spread all over the pathless plateaus.

Kostanjevica Castle

Kostanjevica Castle, one of the largest medieval architectural complexes in Slovenia, has survived the ravages of time and a fire. Restored to its one-time splendour, it now houses a wood-carvers' colony called "Forma Viva"'.

Under the northern slopes of the Gorjanci range, on the Krka river, near the town of Kostanjevica, Bernhard von Spanheim, duke of Carinthia and lord of Carniola, founded the Cistercian

monastery of Sancta Maria in Fontis, "St. Mary at the Wells", in 1234. The monks, brought in from the Carinthian monastery of Viktring (Vetrinj), set to cultivating the marshy ground. By erecting a church in the Cistercian style, they laid the foundation stone of Gothic architecture in Slovenia.

Kostanjevica Monastery — or, as the locals prefer to call it, Kostanjevica Castle — is an outstanding architectural monument, on which we can study the continous growth and development of building styles from Early Gothic through

Renaissance to Baroque. The castle is one of Slovenia's largest medieval architectural complexes; in particular, its arcaded cloisters are by far the largest in the country.

Kostanjevica Castle consists of the church and the adjoining complex of monastery buildings. The church was founded before the mid-13th century, while the monastery complex was still built of wood. It shows the typical ground-plan of a "Bernhardine" Cistercian church, though the basic design was slightly modified in our regions. The Cistercians pioneered the spread of Gothic architectural forms in Europe. So it is understandable that Gothic elements predominate in this building marked by pointed arches and rib-vaults; though traces of the older Romanesque traditions are still apparent.

In the Middle Ages the monastery complex was centred on the cloister. This was originally constructed of wood; only in the 15th century it acquired its fine stone arcades. For a long time the monastery did not extend far beyond the outlines traced by its original ground-plan; but because of incessant raids by Turks and mountain brigands — the Vlahi — it had to be fortified by a system of ramparts and exposed towers. In the 16th century,

however, the building gradually overspilled its original ground-plan, extending southwards. By the progressive addition of new tracts to the south and links with the farm-buildings to the east, a unique arcaded courtyard was created, to serve as the new centre of the living-quarters.

In 1786 emperor Joseph II dissolved the monastery, thus setting an end to its more than 500 years' development. The church furnishings were sold, the church building left to its fate, and a part of the original inner cloister, baroquized by then, was pulled down. In World War II the church and the monastery were ravaged by a fire. Immediately after Liberation, systematic restoration of all sections of the monastery and reconstruction of the church to its pre-1942 shape was taken in hand.

The larger part of the monastery is today transformed into an art gallery, which displays the works of Jože Gorjup, a local painter

and sculptor, France Kralj, graphic artist and painter, and Božidar Jakac, another local painter. There is also a gallery of foreign masters, from the collections of the nearby Carthusian monastery of Pleterje. The surroundings of the castle have been transformed into an open-air gallery of wood-carvings, the "Forma Viva", with the co-operation of leading sculptors from all over the world, who have spread the fame of Kostanjevica both as a centre of modern sculpture and a remarkable monument of architecture.

1 Kostanjevica Castle is one of Slovenia's largest ancient architectural complexes. 2 The wide empty spaces have been dotted with sculptures created by the international wood-carvers' colony called "Forma Viva". 3 The castle allows us to follow the development of architecture from Gothic through Renaissance to Baroque. 4 Modern artistic expression set against a Baroque façade.

Ćele Kula

After their victory over the Serbian rebels on Mount Ćegar, the Turks, by order of the pasha of Niš, constructed a tower from the skulls of the massacred Serbians. This hair-raising monument, called Ćele Kula, once contained 952 skulls.

Since immemorial times travellers from Europe to the Middle East, or from Asia to Europe, had to pass through the valley of the Southern Morava. Not far from the spot where the Nišava joins the Southern Morava, the road forked: southwards, to Macedonia and Greece, and eastwards, to Bulgaria and Asia Minor.

It was at this crossroads, today occupied by the industrial city of Niš, that the Celts founded a fortress called Naissus in the 3rd century B.C. The name was retained by the Romans, whose outpost soon developed into a municipium.

The most famous son of Naissus was the illegitimate child of a Roman army officer and a local tavern-keeper. He was destined to become the Roman emperor Constantine the Great.

In its more than 2000 years' history Niš has witnessed many a historical event, some of which have left lasting traces. One of its monuments may well compete for the title of the world's most hair-raising monument. It is called Ćele Kula, "Tower of Skulls", and is located on the western outskirts of the city.

In spring 1809, during the First Serbian Uprising, about 12,000 rebels advanced from Deligrad in the direction of Niš.

Wary of its fortifications defended by a Turkish garrison, complete with artillery, the insurgents halted at the village of Kamenica, some 10 kilometres from the city. They laid siege to the place, and a savage battle ensued. After a few days the Turks were relieved by a force of 40,000 soldiers, rushed in from Bulgaria and Leskovac. They launched their main attack towards Mount Čegar, held by Stevan Sindjelić, duke of Resava, with 3000 men and 4 cannon. Surrounded by the Turks and unable to resist the onslaught of their far superior forces, he fired his pistol at an ammunition depot, blowing up himself and all his men and causing terrible destruction among the Turks.

By order of the pasha of Niš, the heads of Sindjelić's fallen men were cut, skinned, stuffed with cotton and despatched to Constantinople, while the skulls were used in the construction of a tower, soon to be called Ćele Kula. The skulls were inserted in the outside walls, alternating with bricks: there were 56 rows of 17 skulls each, which makes a total of 952 skulls. The "Tower of Skulls" was not spared by the tooth of time, and most of the skulls have been plundered or destroyed. But the few that remain serve as a gruesome reminder, not merely of the cruelty of the pasha of Niš, but of the atrocity of all wars and killers.

1 Instead of breaking the rebellious spirit of the people, the skulls inserted in the Ćele Kula only helped to rekindle it. 2 The battle of Mount Ćegar — detail from a bas-relief on the monument erected to the defenders.

Trakoščan

Among the hundred-odd castles of Croatia's Zagorje and Prigorje regions, Trakošćan is neither the finest, nor the most authentic. But it fascinates with its well-preserved exterior and its wealth of interior decoration.

Croatia's Zagorje region is a lush green woodland crisscrossed by mountains and hills. It is sprinkled with vineyards and fields and laced by swift brooks and rivulets. The course of the Bednja, hemmed in by wild flowers, threads through the valley, and suddenly widens into little Lake Trakošćan.

Here, mirrored on the lake surface, glorious Trakošćan Castle stands eternally upside-down, twice as large as nature.

Trakošćan is neither the finest, nor the most authentic of the hundred-odd castles of Croatia's Zagorje and Prigorje regions — one could even call it, to some extent, a fake: for some 120 years ago its owner, Djura Drašković, had it reconstructed in the "Norman" style. It was the time of shameless sentimentalism. But under the outside trappings we can still sense the ancient 13th-century stronghold, which once belonged to the counts of Celje, mighty noblemen who ruled almost independently over southern Styria and the western section of Croatian Zagorje. Another owner of the castle was duke Jan Vitovac, who lived in the reign of John Corvinus. At the

close of the 16th century the castle was acquired by the Drašković family, who left here a large gallery of statues, ancient furniture and other treasures, so the whole castle is today converted into a museum, with a concert hall. Hidden deep in the woods, it is a popular resort.

1 Trakošćan is the most picturesque and best-preserved castle of Croatia's Zagorje region. 2 3 The castle has been converted into a museum.

Village Tombstones

The art of Serbia's village tombstones, lined up by the roadside, on hill-tops, in orchards, is as original as the country's folk songs. These soliders' and peasants' graveyards are gruesome chronicles of their times.

Serbia's village tombstones, called "kraj-putaši", are either cross-shaped or form an elongated prism capped by a slab. The face of the monument is usually decorated by a cross, a human figure and an inscription, while the flanks and the reverse are covered by strange designs, ornaments and symbols connected with the life, status and duties of the deceased.

The figure most frequently carved or painted on these tombstones is that of a soldier. Even if the deceased had died as a farmer, tilling his field, or confined to his sick-bed, the village stone-cutter never forgets to add: ex-soldier, brave warrior, who served in that and that unit, took part in that and that battle for his country, won so and so many wounds.

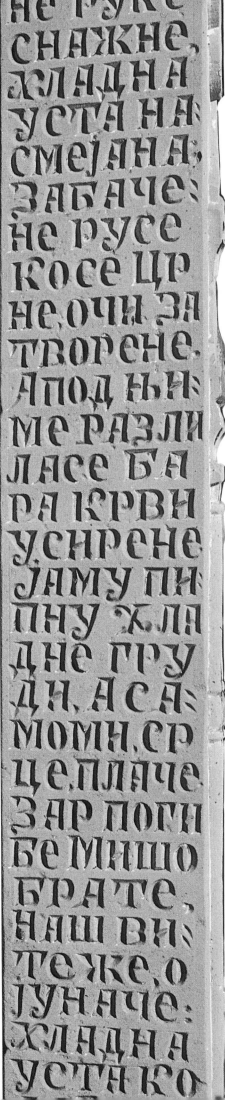

left hand rests on the sword-hilt, while his right hand clutches the cross. The whole figure is cut in a single outline. The eyes are large and bulging, the nose is prominent, the mouth is small, intense, dabbled with a dash of red paint. The youngster seems to emanate an unearthly calm, a self-assurance, as if he had entered true life at last. On the reverse there is an inscription, an ordinary one, resembling the countless other inscriptions designed to arrest the attention of the chance wayfarer: "Come nearer, brother Serbian, and ask God's foregiveness! Here reposes young Ranko Djordjević from Beluša, ex-soldier, who was transported to eternity on 6th December 1876, at the age of 21."

Another village stone-mason chose a joking turn for a tombstone: "Here I repose while you read this; it would have been better if you reposed while I read." There are such graveyards everywhere: by the roadside, in the fields and plum orchards, sprawling on hill-tops, or even buried under the quicksands of rivers. Everywhere the Serbian soldiers seem to stand ghostly guard. The clumsy letters tell us their sketchy biographies. "Stop and look. Here reposes Stojadin Perišić, a brave soldier. He lived before your time, and fought out two wars. In the first he was a sniper, in the second a horse-driver. In the first he pursued the Turks, in the second the Suabians. He gained three wounds: the first left him walking, the second left him breathing, from the third he could never arise again. So he left his bones on the field of glory…" The text may be sad, but the figure on the tombstone shows a merry-maker. Tall, with shaggy eyebrows, sparkling eyes and gaudy cheeks.

These tombstones, erected in the 19th century, now belong to the past.

Serbia's ancient village graveyards, with their unique tombstones, are faithful records of careers, fights, destinies… They stand by the roadside, to escape the most abject of all fates — oblivion.

Serbia's peasants' and soldiers' graveyards are gruesome chronicles of their times. The stone-mason turned chronicler had neither the time, nor the inclination to record scenes from everyday domestic life. War was waged almost incessantly, and the soldiers were the most respected members of the village community.

The fez-covered youngster shown on a monument from 1876 had taken part in the battle of Javor. His figure seems to imply both saintliness and unyieldingness, both revengefulness and righteousness. He looks triumphant, though he had, no doubt, been routed on the battlefield. His

Gem-Like Townscapes

Townscapes delicately chiselled by the ancient master builders can be more beautiful than gems carved by a jeweller's hand: nothing can stale their perfection. They are just as rare as true cameos, and just as capriciously distributed. Indeed, the analogy need not even be pointed out. For what other comparison can do justice to townscapes like Mostar, Dubrovnik, Ohrid…?

Mostar

Dubrovnik

There are scores of other time-stained cities, but there is only one Dubrovnik: a jewel-case transposed into stone, dazzling by the harmony and magnificence of its architecture. It is one of the world's 93 foremost cultural monuments set under immediate UNO and UNESCO protection.

If Venice has been called the queen of the Adriatic, then Dubrovnik is its prince: another city republic with a fabulous history, a hothouse of artistic and scientific genius.
Everything is harmonious here: the great matches the small, the part matches the whole, the foreground matches the backdrop. According to tradition the city was founded in the times of barbarian invasions, by refugees from the nearby Hellenic colony of Epidaurus (today's Cavtat); they established themselves atop the steepest bluff of the little island of Lava

(Laus, Raus, Ragusa, Lit, Litica), which today forms the southern portion of the ancient city core. The settlement soon spilled over the neighbouring heights, and even to a strip on the mainland, at the foot of Mount Srdj, along the channel that linked the little bays of Pile and Ploće. The strait, filled in, became the main thoroughfare of ancient Dubrovnik, the Stradun, or Placa, generally considered one of the world's most beautiful streets. As early as 1301 the city appointed its official physician; in 1317 it set up a pharmacy in the Franciscan monastery; in 1347 it founded the first almshouse, and in 1432 its foundling-hospital. In 1444 the care of disabled servants was discussed by the city councils; and in 1627 the world's first quarantine regulations were passed, to which all travellers and goods from infected countries were subjected, whether arriving by sea or by land — especially those of Middle Eastern provenance.

The patrician republic was headed by the Great Council, the Little Council and the Council of Appeal; all these bodies were accessible only to descendants of ancient noble families. The prince (knez), who was no more than a "primus inter pares", was elected for the term of one year only. Neither slavery, nor serfdom was permitted in the republic. Though the commoners had no say in public affairs, the only monument the republic ever erected to a private citizen was dedicated to a commoner, the merchant and seafarer Miha Pracat, a great benefactor of the city; his statue still stands in the Prince's Palace.

The first urban development plan was introduced by the Statutes of 1272; public records allow us to follow the further expansion and development of the city step by step. Growth was, however, rather cautious and measured, for Dubrovnik's nobility, the "gospari", were suspicious of overhasty changes. They took the greatest pains to introduce the inevitable reforms at a minimum of risk and without endangering the city's chief asset — peace. After the disastrous earthquake of 1667, followed by even more devastating gunpowder explosions — just like after the earlier calamities that had struck the city — the population rallied sufficient energy to heal the wounds, while carefully preserving the city's heritage. The section of the Stradun ravaged by the earthquake was restored to the last detail — at the expense of the republic.

Both their own experiences and the sad fates of other cities had taught the citizens of Dubrovnik a lesson in political cunning: they never lost their instincitve sense of preserving the balance of power in the region. The city sometimes symbolically flew no less than seven foreign flags; but no foreign flag was ever permitted to outshine the white banner of the patron saint of Dubrovnik, St. Blasius, displaying the city's ancient motto, "Libertas". This banner still flutters over the city's Roland's Column at the time of Dubrovnik's Summer Festival.

Crowded in the narrow space enclosed by the city walls, Dubrovnik soon outgrew its shell. Since Baroque times the wealthy citizens, patricians as well as commoners, built their summer villas in the lovely countryside around the city.

Dubrovnik was also a cradle of great men. It is here that the great 16th-century comedy writer Marin Držić was born, and the first opera in any Slav language, J. Palmotić's "Atlanta", was staged. The famous optician Getaldić was a native of the city, while its surroundings gave birth to the mathematician and early champion of the atomic theory Rudjer Bošković, the 18th-century composer Mane Jarnović, and the painter Božidarević.

1 The Stradun, a combination of main street and town square, is the axis of Dubrovnik life. 2 Woman from Konavlje, in the picturesque folk costume of the region. 3 Sponza Palace and the Little Onofrio Fountain — two of the highlights of the Stradun. 4 The ancient city harbour, protected by Fort St. John (Sv. Ivan). 5 The pharmacy in the Franciscan monastery of Mala Braća is more than six and a half centuries old. Overleaf: Dubrovnik from Mount Srdj: a symbol of freedom, and a townscape of unrivalled beauty.

Sveti Stefan

This one-time island fishing-village, fortified by the Paštrovići clan in the 15th century, has been converted into a five-star resort.

Sveti Stefan, on the Montenegro coast, is a rock islet connected to the mainland by a narrow spit of sand.

Watched from the Adriatic Trunk Road, which passes high above, it looks like one of the jewel-studded pendants the local girls wear around their necks for festivals. From sea-level it rather resembles a huge clipper, anchored to the shore by a thin hawser of sand. At night it seems to be sailing at top speed, transporting moonlight through the breakers. The force of the sea and the tooth of time have again and again tried to tear it away from the shore, to sweep it off into the open. But it still resists, firmly clutching the beach, whose chief ornament it is. In spring the bouquet of its red roofs looks rather like the poppies blooming ashore. In winter it rather resembles a pomegranate tree weighed down with ripe fruit.

The solitary island clinging to the coast was fortified by the Paštrović clan from the mainland in the 15th century. They girt it with a loophole-riddled wall. The ancient cannon that still stands at the entrance to the town bears witness of the town's one-time autonomy and strategic importance. The only entrance used to be closed by a heavy iron gate and protected by cannon. Within the battlements the inhabitants put up their stone houses, while the cool cellars served to store their harvests, vintages and other posessions.

Through the centuries, Sveti Stevan was a target for pirates and privateers. According to tradition the inhabitants once captured a pirate ship, with her holds brimful of treasure. As a token of gratitude, they constructed, on the highest elevation of the island, a little church to their patron saint, St. Stephen, after whom the town is still called.

Then the inhabitants began drifting away, and the houses flanking the narrow lanes became deserted. More and more people left, and Sveti Stefan decayed into a ghost town.

In 1955 the conversion into a hotel town began. The lanes, the walls, the roofs, the village square, the ancient façades have all preserved their original appearance; but the interiors are equipped with all the gadgets and conveniences of a de-luxe hotel. So Sveti Stefan, the one-time pirates' target, is now a goal of adventuresome tourists from all over the world.

A pearl-studded pendant dropped in the sea.

Perast

*Boka's seafaring traditions
are centred on Perast,
whose gallant sailors used to circumnavigate the world.
In the 14th century the town housed
a shipyard and one of the first
naval schools on record.
Today it is a Sleeping Beauty.*

Perast is a living monument to the seafaring traditions of the Boka Kotorska. The small, but still glamorous town clings to a rock wall rising almost perpendicularly from the sea; it is built of stone, and on solid stone.

Its churches, its belfries, its palaces, with gorgeously sculptured balconies, rosettes and mullions, used to vie in magnificence and beauty while the town's maritime glory lasted and the sailing-ships continued to bring in treasures. The 17th and 18th centuries.were Perast's golden age, and in the mid-19th century the city still owned 50 large vessels. As early as the 14th century it housed a shipyard, as well as the first naval school of any Slav country.

Little Perast has given birth to a number of famous admirals, who made their careers in various foreign navies, while the great powers used to send their seamen to study navigation at the local naval school. It was from neighbouring Prčanj that captain Ivo Vizin set out on his sailer "Splendido" to circumnavigate the world in a little less than seven years and seven months, the first Yugoslav (or for that matter, the first citizen of the Austrian empire) to achieve this feat.

Sheltered from the north winds and incessantly exposed to the sun, Perast still sails through the times. At every footstep one discovers mementos of its stormy history; but one also notices the tooth of time nibbling away at its age-stained walls. The ivy spreads its roots right into the heart of the masonry, winding up to the ornamented window-sills, gables and belfries. The flowery stone-carvings are gradually submerged by the lush Mediterranean vegetation; Perast, the city of maritime glory, is today a Sleeping Beauty.

luck pointed his cannon at a window and killed his beloved, with whom he now reposes in the same tomb; that of the Perast bride who worked·at her one embroidery for twenty years, patiently waiting for her betrothed to come back from the seas, and at last lost her eyesight; or the career of the famous seaman Peter Martinović, who taught the naval cadets of the Russian tsar Peter the Great.
There is also a legend that tries to explain the origin of the two lovely islands facing Perast: a fleet of stone-laden Turkish ships

Perast's one-time prosperity, fame and greatness can be recaptured at the local museum. Among the exhibits one finds hundreds of objects brought by the citizens of Perast from their ,wanderings: golden chalices and vestments, sea-compasses and etchings of storm-tossed boats, flags and swords, crucifixes and ancient charters, frescos and oil paintings, verses and manuscripts, coats-of-arms daubed on canvas or carved in stone, embroidered silks, ruby and amethyst pendants, gilt silverware…
Many a legend can be recalled here: the story of the grenadeer who by sheer bad

scuttled here in the 17th century. The tradition is revived every year on 22nd July, when stones are brought in by small boats and dropped all around the islands, to strengthen their defences against the waves. Perast's two islets — called St. George and Our Lady of Škrpjel (Gospa od Škrpjela) — form, together with their mountain backdrop, one of the most beautiful scenes imaginable.

1 Returning glory-crowned from the world's oceans, Perast's seamen lavished their treasures on their native town. 2 The islands of St. George and Our Lady of Škrpjel stand guard at the approach to Perast. 3 A stone-carved coat-of-arms.

Trogir

This town, neither on an island, nor on the mainland, but bridging the two, has amassed immense treasure in an area of no more than 20,000 sq. m.; but the finest of all is the portal of its cathedral, carved by master Radovan.

Trogir seems to have been born in the sign of Kairos, the Greek god of lucky chance, whose relief image has been found here. Indeed, the ancient Greeks must have had a lucky hand when they chose this tiny cliff, wedged in between the island of Čiovo and the foothills of Mount Kozjak on the mainland, for the colony they called "Goat Hill" (Tragos oros, Tragouros, Trogir).

The city is one of the exceptional cases of Greek colonies whose ancient genealogy has been preserved. By some lucky chance, the memoirs of its high-priest (hieronymus) have survived, along with a considerable number of hellenistic sculptures. Pliny calls the city "renowned for its marble". And it is in this city that the only existing copy of Petronius's Trimalchion's Feast can be found, still the supreme model of Latin prose.

Even in later times luck was faithful to this cradle of history. Thanks to its protected position the city survived almost unscathed from antiquity right into the Middle Ages. A royal charter, the "Trogir Diploma", granted full communal autonomy to the town. To discourage surprise attacks, the citizens put up a ring of massive battlements and towers, which still stand intact.

Among the many famous buildings, one of the most remarkable is the miniature Ancient Croatian church of St. Barbara, dating from the 9th century, and restored in the 11th century.

The cathedral, with its façade teeming with hundreds of stone figures carved by Master Radovan, is one of the finest Romanesque churches of the Adriatic.

At the southern town gate there is a small loggia, once a shelter for belated wayfarers, today a fish-market.

On the Main Square, flanking the Prince's Palace and the large Gothic loggia, the most outstanding building is the Fanfogna Palace, once a voluminous private library and archive, now housing the City Museum. There is a long list of other important buildings: the Kamerlengo Fortress, the Cipico and Lučić Palaces (the latter being the birth-place of the founder of Croatian scientific historiography), and a Glorietta erected by Marshal Marmont.

1 The city was protected by a ring of battlements and towers. 2 The ancient palaces vie in splendour: the Cipico Palace. 3 Trogir is congested on a cliff between the island of Čiovo and the mainland. 4 Trogir Cathedral is one of the most important Romanesque buildings of the Adriatic. 5 The glory of Trogir is Master Radovan's cathedral portal.

Nin

Here the Liburnians built their biremes, the famous "liburnas". In the early Middle Ages the town was the meeting-place of Croatian tribal chiefs.

Nin is a quiet, unassuming town some 20 kilometres to the north of Zadar. It is situated in a region of fine sands and sweeping expanses of Mediterranean shrubbery, over which the view ranges unimpeded all the way to the mighty Velebit range.

From the slopes of the mountain, the winds carry clouds of fine pollen, which alights on the shore, blending with the even finer golden sands. Through the centuries these deposits have formed into the fertile — and reputedly medicinal — mud of Nin.

In classical antiquity Aenona was a municipium of the Roman province of Liburnia. It was one of the centres of the Liburnians, an Illyrian tribe famous for their seamanship and their prowess at

ship-building. Their biremes, the so-called "liburnas", were outstanding for their manoeuvrability, and served as the prototype of the later Roman triremes, the classical battle-ships of the Roman fleet. Aenona then boasted numerous palaces, a forum, an amphitheatre and a temple consacrated to Diana. Recent research has even given some weight to the tradition that emperor Augustus himself sought cure for his rheumatism or his battle wounds in the local mud-baths. Nin was pillaged in the first wave of Barbarian invasions. The Croats settled here very early, and the place was considered one of their tribal centres. Grgur of Nin, the celebrated "bishop of the Croats", was born and lived here. At the Split Council of 925 A.D. he was the outstand-

ing defender of the use of the vernacular language in liturgy.

Among the Ancient Croatian constructions preserved in Nin the most remarkable are the churches of the Holy Cross (Sv. Križ) and of St. Nicholas, both built on a typical quadrifoliate ground-plan.

1 The church of the Holy Cross (11th century) is a typical Ancient Croatian construction. 2 The church of St. Nicholas surmounts an isolated hill. 3 The "bursa" of St. Marcella. 4 The harbour, 5 Bishop Grgur of Nin, the celebrated defender of the vernacular language.

Istrian Towns

The monument-spangled old towns spread all over Istria preserve the aura of the past centuries.

Istria, the major peninsula of the Northern Adriatic, is a medley of European civilizations. Such a motley mosaic of cultural influences can hardly be encountered anywhere else.

Her number-one showpiece is, of course, Pula, with its fully preserved Roman temple and its mangificent Vespasian's Arena completed in the mid-2nd century, and still capable of holding 30,000 spectators.

All Istria is, in fact, studded with Romanesque, Gothic, Renaissance and Baroque façades, portals and balconies. Here the

spirit of the past centuries survives.

Throughout her three natural zones — the coast, the immediate hinterland, and the hilly interior — Istria offers an unequalled palette of characteristic spatial solutions. There are literally hundreds of fine views and townscapes. No less than thirty of these latter can be experienced by merely skirting the coastline: Kastav, dramatically perched atop the Kvarner Gulf; Volosko, the homely-looking fishing-town and former pirates' nest, clashing with the fin-de-siècle elegance of Opatija, and surmounted by the charming little churches of Mount Veprinac and Mount

Rukavac; venerable Lovran, overshadowed by its ramparts; time-stained Mošćenica, now lost among high-rise hotels; Plomin, with its arches and veands; Labin, poised high up in the skies, and commanding sweeping views from its terraces.

Istria — this is also idyllic Vrsar; Baroque-bedizened Bala, resembling a feverish dream; ancient Poreč, of the fabulous mosaics; Rovinj, with its fishing-fleet; Novigrad, modest, but pleasant; little Umag, white and terraced… Or Barban, Buje, Buzet, Dvigrad, Grožnjan, Motovun, Oprtalj, Tar, Žminj, all huddling within their well-preserved rings of walls and watch-towers, each a maze of little lanes and dreamy courtyards. Kum has been called the world's smallest town: it consists of nothing but its town square. Pazin, the largest inland city, balances on the verge of a precipice, high above the Pazinčica river.

1 Vespasian's Arena in Pula is one of the best-preserved constructions of its kind. 2 A lane in Grožnjan. 3 The hill-top towns rise like watch-towers above the plain: Motovun. 4 Magnificent mosaics: Poreč basilica, founded by bishop Euphrasius. 5 The Istrian ox, renowned for strength, is still irreplaceable.

Škofja Loka

The main charm of this small medieval town is in its manageable, humane proportions.
The bustle of modern life gives meaning to the existence and beauty of the ancient buildings, to the existence and beauty of the urban complex.

Škofja Loka has preserved all the typical traits of a small European city of the Middle Ages: the town walls, the arrangement of the merchants' and craftsmen's houses around the two town squares, the Gothic parish church, and the mighty castle dominating the scene. To a visitor with modern preconceptions it looks rather like a toy city. The houses around the Main Square hardly ever rise beyond the second floor, and if you approach Loka from Ljubljana, along the left bank of the Sora, you can embrace the whole complex at a single glance. If you decide to take a stroll around the city walls — in some places perfectly restored, in other places in need of some repair — it will not take you more than a quarter of an hour. Yet, this town once functioned as a more or less autonomous community, governed by its own city statutes. Here not only the masters of various crafts and the shrewd merchants, but also the modest journeymen, jobbers and servants could live the life of free citizens, protected by the mighty hand of the bishops of Freising, who had founded the town about 1274. Each citizen possessed a house of his own, where he practised his craft or opened his shop. His living space was circumscribed by the city walls. Within them he could carry on his job and acquire everything he presumably needed for life: food, education, the spiritual consolation of religion, a trade or profession, and a bed in the town's almshouse...

The main charm of Loka is precisely in its

the embroidery-like painted friezes. It is only now that the fine portals of green volcanic tuff, which are a typical feature of Loka, have really come into their own. The Main Square has thus re-emerged as a harmonious space, enriched by gay colour accents — a witness to the cheerfulness and love of colour of the bygone centuries. An outstanding example of this ancient gaiety — as well as the ambition to follow the latest mannerist fads of the big cities — is a Late Renaissance house whose owner had the

manageable, humane proportions. Admittedly, many a building in the town shows the hand of expert restorers, and the entire complex is protected as a historical monument; nevertheless, Loka is anything else but a museum exhibit. But the vigorous rhythm of modern economy is here tempered by the nobility of the medieval environment, or vice versa: the bustle of modern life gives meaning to the beauty of the medieval urban complex. The little houses that surround the small square, or rather enlarged street, called "Spodnji Trg" or "Lontrg" show that this was the quarter inhabited by the less

prosperous classes. But the buildings, with their projecting, console-supported first floors, are extremely picturesque.

The wealthier citizens, to be sure, lived in the houses fronting the Main Square. In the times of greatest prosperity, such as the end of the 15th century or certain later ages, they could afford a considerable outward show of luxury. Therefore a walk around the Main Square is a real experience — particularly now the age-old whitewash has been carefully removed from the façades, to disclose the magnificent ancient paintings and ornaments that lay hidden beneath, such as

upper floor painted to give the illusion of an arcade opening on a cloud-studded sky.

The Baroque memorial column in the centre of the square overlooks the bustle that still reigns here, while in the background the ancient Homan house (13th – 16th centuries) closes the view towards the parish church, raised in 1471.

1 Picturesque and self-contained Škofja Loka, though a highly organized urban complex, can be embraced at a glance. 2 3 4 All is made to man's own measure here: the dimensions, the proportions, and even the bright, cheerful colours. Views of the Main Square.

Mostar

There are few cities, ancient or modern, that can boast a landmark as eye-catching as Mostar's Old Bridge, which has defied gravity for centuries, and at the same time look back on such a striking history.

The ancient bridge, spanning the capricious Neretva in a single elegant leap, is the emblem of Mostar. This "kudret kemeri" — miracle arch — is unforgettable.

Mostar derives its name from the "mostari", or bridge guards. Its fate has always been linked with its roads, its bridge, and its garrison safeguarding the river crossing. Everything else is interwoven with this main thread: from the fine old mosques to the avenues of whitish plane-trees, from the dust-stained folios to the moon-lit river, from the source of the Buna and Blagaj Castle to the bustle of the old bazaar, from the sparkling golden "žilavka" of the neighbouring vineyards to the bronze donkey set up in the Main Square as a symbol of the hardships of life in stony Herzegovina.

Indeed, there are few cities that can boast a landmark as eye-catching as Mostar's Old Bridge. It was built in 1566 by Mimar Hajrudin, a well-known master builder, disciple of the famous architect Mimar Sinan. Its single arch is 27.80 metres wide, and almost elliptic in shape. A parapet skirts the paved roadway, and every detail is wrought with care. It is, no doubt, a masterpiece of perfection. Evlija Čelebija, the famous chronicler, was the first to describe it, in 1664: "It looks like a rainbow rising up to the Milky Way, leaping from sheer rock to sheer rock". He adds that the water runs both above and below, since the bridge also serves as an aqueduct. Two towers used to defend it, and underscore its beauty today: the Herceguša, or Tara, on the left bank, and the Halebinovka, or Ćelovina, on the right bank. Both are older than the bridge itself. A stone's throw from the bridge is the ancient Kujundžiluk Bazaar, with its workshops and stalls, its cobbled lanes and its outlooks on the bridge and the daring youngsters diving from it into the rushing Neretva.

But Mostar is, after all, more than its Old Bridge, though everything seems to start from it, and lead back to it.

The town chronicle reaches much further back. Its first page was opened by the archaeologists, who excavated in the Green Cave above the source of the Buna, where hunters of the so-called Mediterranean Culture resorted some 5000 years ago. The Middle Ages are represented by Blagaj Castle, set on a precipitous rock above the Buna: the one-time capital of the "land of Hum", seat of Sandalj Hranić and his nephew and successor Stjepan Kosača (who died in 1466) — the mighty duke ("herceg") Stjepan, after whom the stony region has been named Herzegovina.

An ancient document from Dubrovnik mentions the first settlement on the present site of the city as "due Castelli al ponte de Neretua".

But it was the Turks who gave Mostar its privileged position: in 1522 they transferred here, from Foča, the seat of the sanjak-beg of Herzegovina. They raised numerous important buildings: mosques, public baths, caravansaries. In 1664 the city contained 350 shops. In the 17th century its population exceeded 12,000. It has always been a prosperous city. Here a Pleiad of geniuses — poets and scholars — lived and created lasting works. The

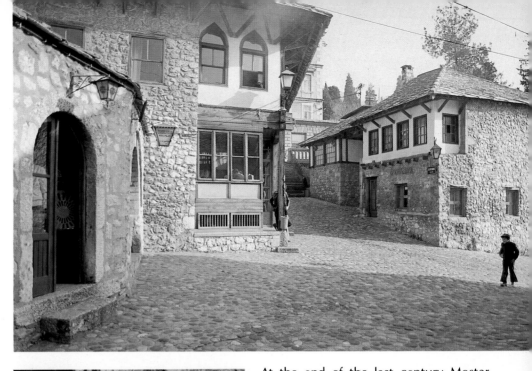

most eminent personality of ancient Mostar was Mustafa Ejubović (1650 – 1707), better known as "sheik Jujo", who achieved the highest honours in Constantinople, but returned to his native town to become its mufti. His interpretations of Islamic law were used for a long time throughout the Ottoman empire. He wrote some 40 books from the fields of law, rhetoric and philosophy.

About 1400 ancient manuscripts from the times before 1878 are preserved in various libraries and archives; they were written by natives of Mostar, mostly in Turkish, Arabic or Persian.

At the end of the last century Mostar resumed its position of focal point of culture. Particularly important was the literary magazine "Zora", first edited by the poet Aleksa Šantić and the writer Svetozar Ćorović, later by Jovan Dučić and Atanasie Šola. Another member of this literary circle was Osman Djikić. The foremost Yugoslav writers of the time contributed to the magazine, which published first versions of some of their major works.

Another important publishing project was the "Mala Biblioteka", launched by the local publishing firm Paher-Kisić; it comprised 185 volumes (110 titles) between 1899 and 1910. Up to the eve of World War II some 1000 titles were printed in Mostar.

A remarkable episode of the Partisan fights of World War II was the secret entry of the survivors of a whole Partisan battalion into the well-garrisoned occupied city. In June 1943 the Mostar Battalion had been reduced to almost half of its strength after the heavy engagements at the Sutjeska during the enemy's Fifth Offensive. Most of the survivors were wounded or ill. So the decision was taken to slip back into the native town! Thus 80 Partisans found their way to the safety of their homes, where they could be nursed back to health. In spite of routine searches the occupiers' police never found them out. When the fighters had taken a good rest and the wounded had recovered, they slipped out of the city again, and the battalion reassembled, to resume fighting.

1 The Old Bridge, rising above the bazaar and flanked by two towers, is a paragon of elegance. 2 Products of the coppersmiths' art. 3 Here two architectural styles blend into one: the oriental and the autochthonous. 4 The source of the Buna: a gushing spring, prehistoric Green Cave, and a dervish monastery.

Počitelj

For centuries this town has stood guard over the Neretva river. Just as unchanged as the river itself, the "old man on the Neretva" has been given a new lease of life by modern restorers.

We ignore the exact date when Počitelj was founded. We only know that somebody, at some time in the grey past, came here, piled stone on stone, and tried to live in peace. History might be silent about it; but the stone pavements, worn by human feet, bespeak that people must have lived here for a long time. Thus the first records of man's presence on the spot are his footsteps; historical documents came much later, when history caught up with the place…

And history first invaded Počitelj when the Turks began their inroads on the land of duke ("herceg") Stjepan. From that moment things started rolling. The name of the place keeps cropping up in official correspondence, in deeds of donation, in ledgers of expenses, on military maps. Master builders, carpenters, stone-cutters, iron-smiths were rushed in to erect a fortified frontier post. Construction went on day and night. It made rapid progress — but so did the Turks.

Počitelj was conquered by a Turkish janissary called Hamza. He put the finishing touch to the half-finished constructions. He fortified the battlements and towers, and transformed the watch-post into a town. Merchants and craftsmen flocked in. Počitelj expanded — though there was not much to expand into, for the place is squeezed in a little hollow between the Neretva and the Karstic heights, like in a Procrustean bed. So it was destined to remain a pocket-size town, guarding the river and the main road skirting it — a collection of tall towers, tiny houses, endless staircases, and lots and lots of stone.

In the evening the town gates were shut, and night had to be spent among its dungeon-like walls. But in those days an iron-spiked gate and a heavy oak bolt were the only guarantees of peaceful slumber. So the stone pavements ceased echoing at nightfall, since nobody even dreamt of walking around at that time. Only the river went on rushing below. And the moonshine trickled down the roofs and towers, staining the stone with the patina of old silver.

It was predominantly an officers' town. One of these Turkish officers, Šišman-pasha, constructed several buildings here. The mosque that still bears his name is like a verse turned into stone. The bell that used to hang in the clock-tower facing the mosque was brought all the way from Crete, where it had pealed in a church. Here, in Počitelj, it chimed in with the prayers from the mosque. It is a mystery who ordered it to be brought over from Greece and why; the journey was immense — but so was the distance at which the chimes could be heard. They were timed by a clock mechanism that was reputed a wonder. Both the bell and the clockwork met a sad end: the former was cast into cannons, while the springs and wheels of the latter finished up as children's toys. What remains is the clock-tower itself: bleak and dumb, like all lifeless things. It has ceased to mark the time; but it would have been difficult to tell the time here anyhow, since the world around has changed through the centuries, while the old guardsman at the Neretva river survives, though with blunted weapons.

The battlements crumbled away one by one. The cupolas of the caravansaries collapsed, and the travellers ceased coming. The glamour of Počitelj paled. There was less and less gold in the purses. The craftsmen left for Stolac and Mostar. The scholars left too — and there had been plenty of them here. Books serving all Bosnia and Herzegovina had been compiled and copied here, and the local scribes could write several foreign languages as fluently as their mother tongue. When larger cities arose in more spacious and more comfortable locations, the lamps of Počitelj went out at dusk, just like in a village; there were less and less people to read and write.

Little by little everything emptied: the shops, the store-houses, the coffers and chests, the mangers, the powder-magazines — and at last the town itself. Only what is eternal subsisted: the lichen-stained stone.

Only an occasional creaking door broke the silence — and the unceasing murmur of the Neretva. For the river had nothing to lose: it could neither change nor grow old...

1 Time had doomed Počitelj to oblivion, but a new road has revealed its beauty. 2 The Gavrankapetanović tower, a vigilant watch-post above the Neretva river. 3 Here everything can be taken in at a glance. 4 House by house has been carefully restored.

Kruševo

The Kruševo Republic lasted no more than 13 days, but it is one of the purple pages in the tortured history of the Macedonian Slavs. The Kruševo Manifesto is a call for unity.

On 2nd August 1903 an attack on the Turkish barracks of Kruševo, signalled by the pealing of bells and a sudden outburst of shooting, marked the beginning of the Ilinden (St. Eliah's Day) Uprising against the Ottoman rulers, who had oppressed Macedonia for five centuries.

At that moment Kruševo, an unpresuming little town 1250 metres above sea-

level, became the capital of the Kruševo Republic — the first ever republic in the Balkans. It was the seat of its government and the residence of its first President, Nikola Karev.

After no more than 13 days the republic was stifled in blood. Its leaders were massacred, and the uprisal was just another purple page in the tortured history of the Macedonian Slavs — a nation that had to wait and fight for its national state longer than any other in Europe.

Kruševo is, along with Ohrid, Kratovo and Veles, an outstanding showpiece of traditional Macedonian town architecture. Though the revengeful Turkish forces set fire to the town after they had quelled the rebellion, the bulk of ancient Kruševo has survived unscathed.

Man here lives face to face with the past. You seem to hear it revive when you walk

the silent lanes; you seem to breathe it in the fresh breezes from its forests, which reach down to the first houses. You listen to the hammering of the last surviving goldsmiths and silversmiths, welding their thin metal wires into dazzling filigree patterns. You stop every now and then to admire some curious detail on an old house, wrought by the hand of some anonymous wood-carver. You bargain for the products of local handicraft, whose designs are often as old as the town itself. And you contemplate the town's leading rebels, as it were, in flesh and blood — turned into statues: Nikola Karev, the First President of the Kruševo Republic; or Pitu Gulija, the rebels' military leader, who took his stand on the Mečkin Kamen above the town, and preferred to perish with all his men rather than leave the town unprotected…

The socialist-inspired Kruševo Manifesto, issued by the Government of the rebel republic on the second day of the uprising, has assured Kruševo a lasting place in the history of socialist movements. It appeals not only to Macedonians, but also to the ethnic groups living among them — even to Moslems, such as Turks and Albanians — to take up arms against the Ottoman oppressors: "We are not pointing our guns at you... Come under the flag of free Macedonia! She is your mother, too. Come and burst the chains of slavery, to free yourselves from pain and suffering... We are going to fight and to die both for yourselves and for ourselves."

1 2 3 Kruševo sprawls cascade-like downslope, or rises staircase-like uphill. 4 A cherry-wood cannon from the Ilinden Uprising. 5 The Macedonium — a modern memorial to the freedom fighters.

Kratovo

The "golden age" of Kratovo began in the 13th century, when its gold mines were reopened, and the town's fame and prosperity continued well into the Turkish period. The Turkish poet Zaifi (16th century) suggests his compatriots should, rather than flock to Mekka, make their pilgrimages to Kratovo, on whose gold they lived.

Kratovo, an ancient Macedonian town north-east of Skopje, is hidden by a ring of volcanic mountains, at the bottom of an extinct crater, from which legend derives its name. It is laid out in the shape of an amphitheatre, with its time-stained timbered houses arranged on a flight of terraces.

What distinguishes this town from all others are its admirable single-span bridges, constructed in the 14th century. In Kratovo's "golden age" there were also five fortified towers, of which only two survive.

The Thracians, hankering after the gold-bearing sands of the Kratovo and Zletovo rivers, were the first tribe to invade this region, which its original Illyrian inhabitants called Paeonia, and to establish a settlement on the site. Kratovo was also known as a mining centre in Roman times; on a map of the period it is marked as "Tranapura".

The 12th-century Arab traveller and geographer Idrisi mentions the town under the name of Kortos, or Koritos, and calls it a "highly developed" city. In 1199 Kratovo is listed in a charter of the Byzantian emperor Alexis III as "Episkopos Koriton".

But the real golden age of Kratovo began in the 13th century, when mining registered an unprecedented boom throughout the Balkans. The Serbian king Milutin, who ruled from 1282 to 1321, conquered the city and brought in miners from Saxony to reopen the mines. The town achieved further progress under the Serbian "tsar" Dušan, whose reign lasted from 1331 to 1355, and the local "gospodar" Oliver; in its heyday the Dejanović brothers established a colony of Dubrovnik merchants here.

The Plavica-Zlatica mountain was then considered the richest goldfield of the Balkans. Several silver and gold coins of that period were minted in Kratovo. A literary school of Kratovo is also on record from the same age.

After the Turkish conquest a 15th-century document points out that the commerce of Edirne, Xeres and Kratovo brought more profits to the Turkish treasury than all the taxes collected in the empire. The 16th-century poet Zaifi suggests his compatriots should, rather than flock to Mekka, make their piligrimages to Kratovo, on whose gold they lived. The Venetian traveller Catarino Zeno registers that the Kratovo mines yielded the sultan 70,000 ducats per year. Konstantin Jireček states that Kratovo was, in the 16th century, one of the richest towns of the European section of the Ottoman empire. In the 17th century Kratovo lodged no less than 350 workshops and commercial firms, which traded with Dubrovnik and Constantinople. In 1660 the chronicler Evlija Čelebija records that Kratovo boasted 20 churches and two public steambaths, of which one could compete with the very finest establishments of Constantinople and Damascus. When the Austrian forces, launching an attack at the Turks, advanced all the way to Skopje, the miners of Kratovo staged an uprising against the Ottoman rulers. Recapturing the city, the Turks massacred its inhabitants, and of the ancient glory only the fabulous bridges and the two towers remain. Another distinguished survivor is the nearby monastery of Lesnovo, once the seat of a literary school.

1 Stone bridge from the 14th century. **2** Kratovo, located at the bottom of a volcanic crater, was a "golden town"; in the 16th century it was one of the richest cities of the Ottoman empire.

Prilep

In the turmoil of the early Middle Ages a Slav tribe, the Brsjaci, withdrew from the plains of Pelagonia, to establish a new town on the mountain spur called Markove Kule.

The origins of medieval Prilep reach back to the second half of the 9th and beginning of the 10th centuries. In that time of turmoil, when Byzantium and Bulgaria waged savage fights for the possession of this region, the inhabitants of the Pelagonian plain — the Slav tribe called Brsjaci — were compelled to abandon their unprotected lowland settlements and make for the hills, where they established a chain of mountain fastnesses.

In the stormiest period of the medieval history of the Macedonian Slavs, during the reign of the Macedonian "tsar" Samuel (976 – 1014), one of our largest medieval towns arose on the southern and north-western slopes of the Markove Kule heights. The imposing ruins preserved on the site give evidence of a well-established Slav architectural tradition. The walls and roofs were constructed of timber, wattle-and-daub, and straw thatch. The provisions were kept in niches cut in solid rock, or in wooden sheds. There were stone mortars, querns and kneading-troughs. The ground-plan of the settlement shows four distinct zones. The largest of these was the residential area proper. The highest summit was probably dominated by a small fortress. On the south-eastern flank of the mountain there was an extensive necropolis dating from the turn od the 9th and 10th centuries. At the foot of the hill a community centre was laid out, with a rock-hewn throne. After the collapse of Samuel's empire, in 1014, the strategical reasons that had led to the establishment of the fortified town ceased to exist, and the inhabitants gradually moved into the plain, to the site of the present-day village of Varoš.

Another turning-point for the development of medieval Prilep was reached in the mid-12th century, when the Byzantian authorities settled a new, non-Slav population in the region. The newcomers were not atracted by the mountain fastness of Markove Kule. They used building materials and techniques unknown to ancient Slav architecture. Their lowland city reached its economic and cultural heyday in the second half of the 13th and first half of the 14th centuries. Then decline set in, to last for ages.

1 Legend connects the ruins of the medieval city with the folk hero Prince Marko; it is, in fact, much older, and has proved a treasure-trove of archeological finds. 2 A whim of nature: the stone elephant. 3 The warmth of closed space: a city backyard.

Ohrid

*For long centuries Ohrid
was a gathering-place of writers,
philosophers, theologians,
philologists, painters
and patrons of art;
the lakeside city is thus
a unique treasury of spiritual
and material gems.*

The political, and above all, cultural role of medieval Ohrid is closely connected with the activity of St. Clement (Sv. Kliment) of Ohrid, the most famous disciple of the Slavonic apostles St. Cyril and St. Methodius.

After his expulsion from Greater Moravia, Clement found, in 886 A. D., a safe refuge on the shores of Lake Ohrid. Here he established the centre of Slavonic literature and set the foundations of the literary school of Ohrid. The oldest surviving codices in Glagolitic script, on parchment, date from his time. Through them we can follow the development of the ancient

Slavonic language. Clement himself wrote no less than 42 books on religious or educational topics.

Clement also constructed the monastery church of St. Panteleimon (about 893 A. D.), to a trifoliate ground-plan. A few years later his closest collaborator, St. Nahum (Sv. Naum) of Ohrid, erected the monastery church of the Holy Archangel, today's Sv. Naum.

According to Theophilact of Ohrid, more than 3000 pupils graduated from Clement's school, to spread Slavonic literature into numerous countries, even into Kiev Russia. Slavonic letters experienced a second bloom during the reign of the Macedonian "tsar" Samuel, when Ohrid became the political centre of an independent state, while the church of Ohrid was granted jurisdiction over the greater part of the Balkans.

After the fall of Samuel's empire (1018 A. D.) and the re-establishment of Byzantian rule, Ohrid was made an archbishopric, whose territory spread from Southern Macedonia all the way to the Danube and the Adriatic. A succession of eminent men occupied the archiepiscopal see of Ohrid: writers, philosophers, patrons of art, scholars of classics and divinity. Some of them achieved prominence in medieval cultural and political history. Leo, the founder and protector of St. Sophia Monastery, played a decisive role in the schism between the Eastern and Western churches (1054). Theophilact of Ohrid, a brilliant stylist, wrote a voluminous "Life of St. Clement". Demetrius the Homatian, foremost expert on ecclesiastical law, defended the autonomy of the Church of Ohrid.

In the mid-11th century the cathedral church of St. Sophia was decorated with frescos. They are painted in the monumental style of the Macedonian dynasty, and form the most comprehensive fresco complex of the period preserved anywhere in Europe.

This laid the foundations of Ohrid as a city of art. In the late 13th century the "zoographers" Michael and Eutychius, leading fresco painters of the Paleologue Renaissance, accepted a major commission in Ohrid. Their frescos in the church of St. Mary Peribleptos (today's St. Clement), dating from 1296, are the first monument of the new age in Byzantian painting.

Ohrid's numerous well-preserved 14th-century frescos can give us an idea of the destroyed artistic complexes of contemporary Constantinople and Thessaloniki. Both under Byzantian rule and under the mantle of the Serbian "tsar" Dušan and the local "gospodars" a number of painters set up their workshops in the city. Ohrid's greatest master, John the Theorian (mid-14th century), inspired a crowd of pupils, who were to dominate the artistic life of the city and its archbishopric for a long time afterwards.

In the 18th century the movement for the restoration of these artistic treasures set in. The city's merchant class and ecclesiastical circles thoroughly reconstructed the monastery complex and church of St. Nahum, which was furnished with a Baroque iconostasis; a new archiepiscopal palace was erected, and the lives of the Macedonian saints were re-edited.

After 1830, when the Turkish administration was liberalized, several large churches were raised or reconstructed in pre-Renaissance style.

The medieval core of Ohrid was given a new, orderly appearance: on the outside the new buildings imitated the ancient architecture typical of the city.

1 The church of St. John the Theologian (Sv. Jovan Bogoslov Kaneo) from the 13th century. 2 The austere outside shell belies the wealth of interior decoration: the apse of St. Clement's (13th century). 3 St. Sophia's preserves Europe's largest surviving 11th-century fresco complex. 4 St. Nahum's (15th to 16th centuries). 5 A masterpiece of residential architecture: the National Museum.

Cetinje

The history of this city,
founded on a barren Karstic
plateau in 1482, is a succession
of glorious feats.
Even the lead type from
the printing house and the lead roof
of the monastery had to be melted
down into bullets.

Cetinje is only a decade younger than its prize museum exhibit, the "Octoich"; yet it has subsisted on its barren plateau for five long centuries. Since 1482, when the foundation stones were laid for a residence of Ivan Crnojević, ruler of Zeta, its chronicle has recorded many a prodigious feat. It has braved the thunder and lightning of Mount Lovčen, the Mediterranean rainstorms from the coast, and the snow-drifts from the interior. And of course, it has repelled invasion after invasion.
Cetinje is situated in a rock-strewn basin, resembling a giant amphitheatre destined for hair-raising spectacles and resounding

speeches. Montenegro's great poet, Njegoš, here first tried out the resonance of his high-sounding verses on the universe, the native country, freedom and humanity.

The city counts hardly more than 10,000 inhabitants, but the documents in its museum show-cases, the books in its libraries and the paintings in its galleries can be counted in millions. For this is a museum town. Hemmed in by the Boka Kotorska and Lake Skadar, by the open sea washing the Montenegrine Coast and the "petrified sea" of the Karst, it overbrims with treasures of human creativity. The city was already crowned with glory while its roofs were of thatch and its books printed in gold; when the lead type of its printing house and the lead roof of its monastery had to be melted down into bullets. When its stock reply to all enemy threats was: "If it is God's will, our stone will be your grave! We have nothing else to tell you. We are awaiting you day and night, for who dies as a free man, has lived enough!" For centuries, to the close of World War I, Cetinje was the capital of an independent little country.

Naturally enough, Cetinje has always attracted the attention of the world. At the turn of our century the European powers used to vie with one another for the finest embassy building. In those times the city boasted no less than ten embassies and consulates, and several daily papers.

Another glorious period in the city's history was the time of World War II, when 5000 inhabitants left for the Partisans; 823 of them never returned, and 49 were proclaimed Resistance Heroes.

1 2 Cetinje is full of surprises: its forbidding setting of grey stone contrasts with the glamorous interiors of its palaces. 3 Crown of the Serbian medieval king Stephen of Dečani (Stefan Dečanski). 4 Cetinje's monastery had to sacrifice its lead roof, to be melted down into bullets. 5 The city has always had to defend its freedom: the Billiards Palace. 6 The National Museum — one-time Royal Palace. 7 The Crnojević coat-of-arms on a capital.

Treasure-Houses

They are incarnations of man's most luminous dreams: shimmering phantasmagorias of miraculous forms and sublime messages, the sum of innumerable experiences and concentrated creative endeavours.
Such treasure-houses of the spirit fascinate us by their noble exteriors, their arhitecture, and sheerly overwhelm us by the wealth of their interiors, their icons and frescos of saints, so surprisingly lifelike and human, their gold and silver wrought by masterly hands, their books penned by self-sacrificing hands...

Iconostasis in the church of the Holy Saviour, Skopje

Churches and Monasteries

The sacred architecture and mural painting of medieval Macedonia and Serbia comprise an inestimable cultural heritage. The churches and monasteries of Ohrid mark the Macedonian beginnings. They were followed by the three architectural schools of Serbia: those of Raška, Kosovo and Morava.

The sacred architecture of medieval Serbia and Macedonia developed as a succession of architectural schools, combining local traditions with both Eastern and Western influences.

The intense architectural activity set in with the acceptance of Christianity by the Macedonian Slavs, chiefly in the times of St. Clement and St. Nahum (at the turn of the 9th and 10th centuries), and reached its first climax in the reign of the Macedonian "tsar" Samuel (in the late 10th and early 11th centuries). In Ohrid St. Clement erected the monastery of St. Panteleimon, now lost under the foundations of Imaret Mosque, while at the southern end of Lake Ohrid St. Nahum founded the church of the Holy Archangel, today partly excavated beneath the later monastery church of St. Nahum (Sv. Naum). The same period also brought a few basilicas, like the church of St. Achilles, on the island of the same name in Little Lake Prespa, or Ohrid's St. Sophia, a three-naved basilica dominated by a single cupola. Though this latter building, evidently conceived as a cathedral, cannot be exactly dated, it was presumably raised under "tsar" Samuel, to be reconstructed by archbishop Leo (probably about 1037 – 1056).

Other fine buildings from the times of Byzantian rule are the monastery church of St. Panteleimon in the village of Nerezi, just outside Skopje (1164), a cross-shaped construction with five cupolas, remarkable for its harmonious proportions; the church of St. Mary Peribleptos, today's St. Clement, in the city of Ohrid (1295), built on the ground-plan of a Greek cross, with a single cupola and decorative polychromous façades of combined stone and brick; the single-naved village church of Kurbinovo, above Lake Prespa (1191); Treskavec Church near Prilep; St. Nicholas Church in Varoš, a suburb of Prilep (1299), with an exceptionally colourful façade; and many others. Under Turkish rule the construction of Christian sacred buildings was halted; only small single-naved churches of modest arhitectural value continued to shoot up sporadically.

In Serbia architecture experienced its first bloom in the second half of the 12th century, in the reign of Stevan Nemanja. In this most significant period of Serbian medieval architecture the kings and feudal lords vied with one another in erecting monasteries and churches as their personal foundations, often in sites outstanding for lovely scenery and picturesque views.

One of the earliest achievements of the »Raška school« is the church of St. Nicholas near Kuršumlija (1168 – 1172). It is Nemanja's own foundation, and its architectural features and techniques are well within the orbit of Byzantian influence. On the other hand, the church of Djurdjevi Stupovi at Ras, near Novi Pazar, today a heap of ruins, shows Western influences, which are even more pronounced in St. Mary's Church of Studenica Monastery (1183 – 1191). This is one of the finest Serbian churches: its façades are patterned in grey and white marble, while its Romanesque portals and windows are framed with bas-reliefs. The most outstanding of the later productions of the "Raška school" are: Žiča (1217), Mileševa (1234), Sopoćani (1264), Gradac (reconstructed about 1270) and Arilje (1295). By its interesting architectural arrangement and the wealth of its relief sculpture the monastery church of Visoki Dečani, erected between 1327 and 1335, is one of the glories of Serbian architecture; it is a five-naved basilica with a single apse and a single cupola. In the 14th century the "Kosovo school" made its appearance. It marked a return to pure Byzantian traditions, both in ground-plan, construction methods and decoration. The buildings of this group are distinguished by either one or five cupolas, and by colourful façades of stone, brick and ceramic decorations.

The most important achievements of the "Kosovo school" are the churches of St. Mary Ljeviška, in the city of Prizren, and of Gračanica, near Priština; the latter was raised about 1318, and is one of the finest and best-preserved monuments of Serbian medieval architecture.

The times of Turkish penetration into the Balkans saw the rise of a third stylistic trend, the "Morava school", which was a synthesis of the two preceding orientations, combined with influences from Mount Athos.

When the Serbian "despotate" at last succumbed to the Ottoman onslaughts, the construction of Christian sacred building was restricted, in this region as well, to smaller, unpretentious churches, which helped to keep tradition alive, but could never hope to reach the pinnacles of the "golden age".

1 The Patriarchal Church of Peć set the pattern for the medieval architecture of Kosovo. 2 Gračanica, a foundation of the Serbian king Milutin, features a profusion of exceptional frescos. 3 Manasija was protected by a ring of battlements. 4 Nerezi is one of the oldest monasteries. 5 This Studenica church is an example of the Morava school. 6 The monastery of Sv. Jovan Bigorski, in the wild canyon of the Radika, preserves Macedonia's finest woodcarvings.

Icons

Yugoslavia is, beyond doubt, one of the world's richest treasure-houses of icons. The Macedonian collection, the most distinguished of all, is dominated by the icons of Ohrid.

The regions of Serbia and Macedonia that remained longest within the orbit of Byzantine culture have preserved this artistic tradition almost into our own time. Icon painting represents an independent branch of Byzantine art, though its artistic approach was sometimes identical to that of fresco painting; at other times, again, it departed radically from the techniques of mural painting, or even assumed a pioneering role.

Though panel painting was also known to some earlier civilizations, it was only in Byzantine times that it assumed the complex, spiritualized character that is, in a way, synonymous with Byzantium. The icon was something more than a mere commemorative picture; it was the chief devotional object of Eastern Christianity, and through its sacred subject matter the believers established an intimate communication with the world of the Lord.

When the Slav peoples of the Balkans accepted Christianity in the second half of the 9th century, the eastern section of the peninsula fell under the spell of Byzantine culture and art. The Slavs soon profoundly assimilated it, and began actively participating in the common development.

Through the ages, several magnificent collections of icons arose on the territories of Macedonia and Serbia; some were painted by the foremost Byzantine masters, others by local artists. Though a considerable number of icons have perished through the centuries, the surviving Yugoslav stock can be counted among the world's most outstanding collections, equal to those of Mount Sinai, Mount Athos and Russia.

Among Yugoslavia's treasure-houses of icons, the Macedonian collection, dominated by the icons of Ohrid, certainly deserves pride of place. There is hardly any other country where we can follow the continuous development of icon painting through almost a millennium, from the first half of the 11th to the late 19th centuries.

1 "Annunciation", Ohrid, early 14th c. 2 "Christ Pantocrator", donated by Constantine Kavasilas, archbishop of Ohrid, in 1262. 3 "Christ's Descent to Limbo", Ohrid, eighties of the 14th c. 4 "Mother of God", Ohrid, first two decades of the 14th c. 5 "Crucifiction", first decade of the 14th c. 6 "Christ", church of the Assumption, Mohovo, 18th c., today at the Matica Srpska Gallery, Novi Sad.

Carvings

The iconostases in the church
of the Holy Saviour, Skopje,
and in Bigorski Monastery
near Debar
are the crowning achievements
of the glorious
Macedonian wood-carving school
of the 19th century.

The tradition of wood-carving is deeply
rooted in Macedonia; numerous carved
doors, pulpits and iconostases grace her
churches and monasteries. The names of
their creators are usually unknown; but
they show an exceptional wealth of artistic invention and a high level of technical
mastery.

The iconostases in the church of the Holy

Saviour (Sv. Spas), Skopje, and in Bigorski
Monastery near Debar are true masterpieces of carving. Both have been produced by the same group of masters
active in the first half of the 19th century
and led by Petar Filipovski, his brother
Marko Filipovski, and Makarije Frčkovski,
all from the village of Galičnik.

The iconostasis (icon-bearing partition
between the altar and the nave) of the
church of the Holy Saviour (1819 – 1824)
is one of the most celebrated carvings
anywhere. It is certainly not one of the
largest (it measures 10 metres in length,
and one story in height), but it outranks all

achievement of the workshop. In this iconostasis, too, the masters have given a prominent position to their own portraits. Stylistically the iconostases of Skopje and Bigorski Monastery are related to the wood-carvings of Mount Athos; it was through this source, no doubt, that Baroque forms found their way into the creations of the Macedonian masters, who instilled them with an exuberance all of their own.

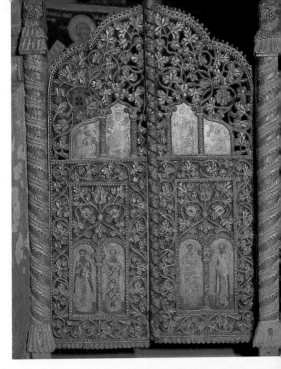

1 Detail from the superb carved iconostasis in the monastery of Sv. Jovan Bigorski, a creation of master Petar Filipovski and his companions. 2 The delicate carving almost resembles miniature-painting. 3 Detail from the iconostasis in the church of the Holy Saviour, Skopje.

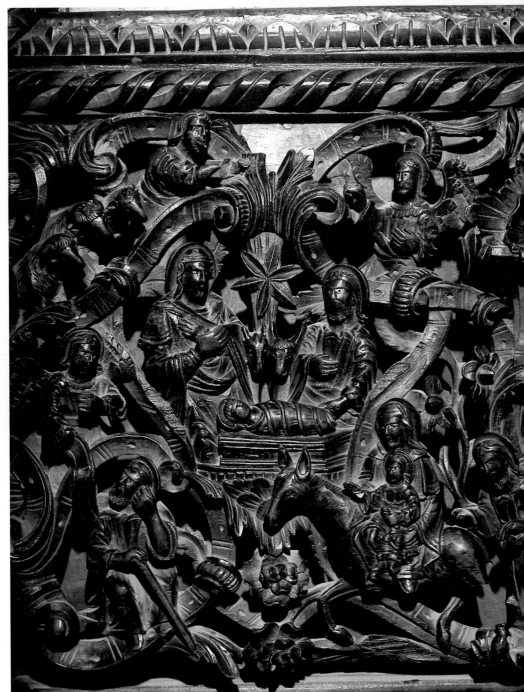

others by its technical perfection, its brilliant composition, and its wealth of vegetal, animal and geometrical ornaments. Masterfully exploiting the peculiar traits of walnut, the carvers have produced a complete cycle of illustrations to the Bible. At the same time they have reproduced the real world as they saw it: in some scenes the figures wear costumes from the carvers' native village.

The iconostasis in the church of Bigorski Monastery (1830–1835) is considerably larger than its Skopje counterpart, two-storied, and even more delicately carved; indeed, it can be considered the crowning

Frescos

The monumental wall-paintings of the churches and monasteries of Macedonia, Serbia and Montenegro are among our most precious artistic heirlooms.

The first major monument — the frescos of St. Sophia's, Ohrid — keeps well within the framework of Byzantine tradition. The 11th century was a time when the icono-

graphic scheme and the arrangement of frescos within the church building had achieved a certain rigidity: a three-zone division both in height and in depth. The lowest sections of the walls were reserved for personalities of this world, the central plane for the miraculous world of the Bible, and highest zone for the Kingdom of Heaven. The closed space about the altar was intended for liturgical rites; the nave, accessible to the faithful, was painted with scenes from the Gospels; while the porch, where the neophytes were confined, featured the horrors of the Last Judgement.

After some interruption, the trend continues through Nemanja's Djurdjevi Stubovi and Kurbinovo to Studenica, whose monumental paintings already show a pronounced local stamp. It was the time when Serbia took the lead over Crusader-ravaged Byzantium. Preserved fragments from Žiča and from St. Nicholas Church near Kuršumlija, as well as the Radoslav Porch in Studenica, confirm this estimate. They all lead up to one of the greatest creations of the medieval world: the frescos of Mileševa. Though unequal in concept and varied in style, they excel by their monumentality and intellectual sub-

tlety: they look rather like the Ravenna mosaics turned into living flesh. In the well-known fresco of the "White Angel" the angel's wide-open eyes seem to announce the rediscovery of this world and the human individual. Mileševa also preserves another fascinating fresco: "St. Mary and the Annunciation".

1 "Prayer on the Mount of Olives", church of St. Mary Peribleptos, Ohrid, 1295, by the painters Michael and Eutychius. 2 "Expulsion from the Temple", church of St. Nikita near Skopje, about 1320, by the painters Michael and Eutychius. 3 "The Last Supper", church of St. Mary, Studenica Monastery, 1568.

This development leads to the archaic "Apostles" in the Patriarchal Church of Peć, which also features a highly unusual "Assumption", where the Virgin looks rather like a healthy, sturdy peasant girl. The frescos of Morača represent a further step towards the discovery of human traits behind the theological subject; then the climax of this humanist trend is achieved in the painting of Sopoćani. The period reaches a dead end with the decadence of Gradac and Arilje. After the re-emergence of Byzantium as a world power new impulses irradiate from there. It is the style of the so-called "Paleologue Renaissance", already presaged by the frescos of Ohrid's St. Mary Peribleptos at the end of the 13th century. The transition period is marked by the wall-paintings in the church of St. Mary Ljeviška, Prizren. Gračanica is a further version of this style, which embroiders the scenes and elaborates on the stories with somewhat excessive love of detail, but a highly picturesque colouring. Nagoričino near Kumanovo, St. Demetrius in Peć, and a sequence of other monuments complete the mosaic of this school, which is often heterogeneous in style, but unified in content. In Dečani this painting achieves a strange transformation and decline, in an all-too-apparent attempt to escape from the shackles of a rigid artistic school,

thouh at the same time remaining within its orbit.

The third great period of this medieval tradition is the painting of the so-called "Morava school" at the turn of the 14th and 15th centuries, in a revived Serbian state, whose centre of gravity had shifted far to the north.

The motif of the "Holy Warriors" is already an important theme in Ravanica, where the painters insist on emphasizing the youthfulness of the figures, endowing them with a lyrical, almost feminine sensibility. In Kalenić the famous "Wedding at Cana" is a faithful rendering of a nobleman's court of Morava-period Serbia. The final chord is sounded by the paintings of Manasija: it is a solemn note, which seems to have been transferred from the ascetic façades to the murals within. The Turkish flood was swooping down on Serbia, and the "Holy Warriors" on the walls of Manasija were to remain the last knightly farewell of the Balkans to troubadour Europe.

1 "Descent from the Cross", church of St. Panteleimon, Nerezi near Skopje, 1265—1268. 2 "Judas's Betrayal", church of St. Mary Peribleptos, Ohrid, 1295, by the painters Michael and Euthychius. 3 "Queen Simonida", Gračanica Monastery, 1321. 4 "Death of St. Mary", church of Sopoćani Monastery, about 1265. 5 "St. Peter", Žiča, about 1316. 6 "Holy Warriors" (detail), Dečani Monastery, 1335—1350.

The White Angel

The famous 13th-century fresco of the White Angel owes its preservation to the fact that it was overpainted, three centuries later, by another master's version of the theme.

Mileševa Monastery, in South-Western Serbia, not far from Prijepolje, was founded by King Vladislav about 1230, while he was still a prince. He called in masters from Constantinople, Thessaloniki and other Byzantian art centres to paint the frescos of the monastery church.

The frescos of Mileševa, along with their somewhat later counterparts of Sopoćani, belong to the most precious artistic creations of medieval Serbia.

The painting of Mileševa can be represented, better than by anything else, by the virtuoso fresco of the "Angel at Christ's Tomb", a version of the Biblical story of the encounter between the angel and the two women visiting Christ's grave. The angel's face is shown radiant with light, and his raiments as white as snow.

Like all true artistic creations through the centuries, the Mileševo fresco has outgrown the religious motivations that had given rise to it. The fresco disarms the beholder by its masterly drawing, its colour harmony, its arrangement of figures, and above all, by the suggestivity of its central figure, the White Angel. To stress his importance, the painter shows him, according to Byzantian convention, larger than the two women and the Roman soldiers dozing at the tomb. The Angel's figure is recoiling in terror; but it holds the centre of attention. This youthful being reminds one of the sculptures of classical antiquity, which represent their subjects in the bloom of ideal beauty. The fresco painter of Mileševa has apparently learnt his lesson from antiquity; but as he was engaged in the service of Christian religion, he has instilled his creation with a new understanding of the co-existence between form and spirituality. Therefore the "White Angel", as the fresco has been called after its dominant figure, is not only a painting of exceptional virtuosity, but also irradiates true inner beauty and a peculiar charm.

In the 16th and 17th centuries the Mileševa frescos were old and damaged. In places the whitewash had crumbled away, in other places the colours had faded. Tiny flakes of gold leaf had peeled off from the mosaic-like backgrounds. Therefore the enterprising monks engaged a painter to overpaint most of the old frescos with new versions of the same themes — among them the "Angel at Christ's Tomb". Fortunately the new painter simply applied a new layer of lime-plaster priming over the old frescos, without damaging them. As the new whitewash did not hold well, it gradually crumbled away or was detached by inquisitive visitors or art scholars. Of the overpainted fresco only a narrow strip at the top remains, as a witness to the questionable taste of the period. But in their time these later paintings served to protect the ancient masterpieces and arrest their further decay, since the church was left roofless for some two hundred years (throughout the 18th and 19th centuries).

This Mileševa fresco carries a universal artistic message.

137

СꙊЩЕНІЄ Ѡ БꙊЄПЇ СТЕ ВНЬ

сщённый и ꙗжⷮтⷡнный правилъ .

потроуженно въкоупѣ, неложен꙯ .
иже въсщенно иноко ꙣ послѣⷣнымъ .
маⷴ.ѳе Ємь солоунескымъ : ·
въ н законикь изѣбраемо . изъвѣ
лїега законника . ꙗковъ скорѣ
ѡбрѣтати нскома ѡвъ саꙗконⷶ
въ ꙣⷩи . и ѡ винн꙯ грѣⷯовныхъ ·

The printing plant had been brought over from Venice by George Crnojević, prince of Montenegro. The printing house was located next door to the church, within the fortress raised by George's father and predecessor on the throne, Ivan Crnojević. The printers were monks; one of them, named Makarije, composed the type of the "Octoich", which some eight of his companions took a whole year to print.

The "Octoich" is one of the liturgical books of Eastern Christianity. It contains hymns corresponding to eight weekly cycles. Each week the anthems are sung in a different tune, or "voice". This explains the Greek title of the collection: "octoichos" means "eight-voiced". The original compilation was mostly done in the 8th century, and includes poems by Damascene, Anatolius, Constantine Porphyrogenetus, and other Byzantian hymn writers. For centuries the manuscript had been copied by hand: following the tradition of the copyists, the Obod edition is divided in two volumes.

Šafařik, the well-known 19th-century bibliophile, called the edition "the most beautiful specimen of Cyrillic print", while the poet and travel writer Ljuba Nenadović declared that "no contemporary book anywhere in Europe surpasses the beauty of the incunabula printed in Montenegro".

A total of six titles were printed at Obod. Then the Obod printing plant was transferred to Cetinje, where it soon went out of business. Later on, in the 19th century, the poet and ruler Njegoš bought new printing machinery.

1 3 "The most beatiful specimen of Cyrillic print" (Šafařik). 2 Obod — location of the first printing house among the Southern Slavs.

Obod

In 1493 the first printing plant among the Southern Slavs was imported from Venice to Obod. It served to print six titles, of which the most famous is the "Octoich", one of Europe's finest incunabula.

The fortress of Obod rises above a picturesque fiord of Lake Skadar and the fishing village of Rijeka Crnojevića. It is here that the first book in Cyrillic script was printed in 1493 and 1494, just a year after the discovery of America. The edition was a compilation of liturgical texts called "Octoich".

стю · а · но

въ

ьш · къ

пѕалма

ѱлани

нєкли

ауюсє

The Miroslav Gospel

This rare 12th-century manuscript on parchment is not only the foundation-stone of Serbo-Croatian literature, but also, due to its splendid illuminations, a real artistic creation. It underwent some strange adventures: from Sv. Petar near Bijelo Polje it strayed to Mount Athos and Corfu, to end up in the Belgrade National Museum.

While the first Serbian state throve under the firm hand of its creator, Stevan Nemanja (who ruled between 1170 and 1196), the princes and other feudal lords followed the example set by the sovereign, founding their own churches and monasteries.

Nemanja's brother Miroslav, prince of Hum, founded the monastery of St. Peter (Sv. Petar) near Bijelo Polje: an austere stone building with a tall white belfry.

In the silence of this monastery the monk Gligorije, with some assistants, spent day after day, night after sleepless night compiling and copying ecclesiastical texts. To glorify the founder of the monastery, they compiled a Gospel synopsis named "The Miroslav Gospel".

For a long time it was uncertain how many monks had taken part in the production of this manuscript. Only in our own century scholars have definitely established it must have been written by Gligorije himself and an unnamed amanuensis. The book is intended for liturgical use in the Eastern church. Though it is an extensive Gospel compilation, it does not contain the complete texts of the four evangelists. It consists of two parts: the first narrates the story of the Passion, while the second is arranged as a calendar. The most precious feature of the manuscript are its illuminations. Gligorije, straining his eyes in the flickering candle-light, spared no pains and toil to conjure up, by his interplay of red and gold, a world of heavenly splendour.

The Miroslav Gospel was only rediscovered at the beginning of the last century. Like many other church treasures, it had somehow found its way to the monastery of Chilandar, the foundation of Serbian kings on Mount Athos. The well-known Russian explorer of Slavonic antiquities, Porphyry Uspenski, stumbled upon the manuscript during his stay at the monastery, and tore out a page for his private collection. It was only in 1896 that the Miroslav Gospel was presented to the Serbian king Alexander Obrenović; so it could at last return to its home country. In 1915, when Belgrade was evacuated in face of the invading Austro-Hungarian forces, the manuscript was transferred to the island of Corfu, from where it was brought back to Serbia at the close of World War I.

The book comprises 181 page spreads on fine white parchment, worn thin in places. The text is arranged in two columns. The wooden case, with a cover of dark leather, was produced by the master bookbinders of the 15th and 16th centuries. The cover is blocked with the monogram of St. Paul, in Greek letters. Today the precious manuscript is one of the star exhibits of the Belgrade National Museum.

In the reign of Miroslav, prince of Hum, the monk Gligorije and his anonymous assistant penned this fine manuscript, highlighting the text with exceptional miniatures.

Aladža Mosque

Foča's Aladža Mosque, built in 1550, derives its name, "the Variegated", from its interior decoration of varicoloured stripes. Tradition reports it was erected by the sultan's inspector of mines, Hasan Čelebija, on the spot where he had been reunited with his mother.

If Sarajevo could boast its riches, Mostar its sages, Livno its fine horses, Banja Luka its accomplished singers, then Foča could take pride in its well-tempered sabres and yatagans... The armourers of Foča were renowned throughout the empire; their "fočankas" were considered equal to the "damascenes" produced in Damascus.

But the finest master this city has ever seen was certainly the architect who conceived its Aladža Mosque, one of the glories of Bosnia. The architect was called Ramadan-Aga, and was one of the disciples of the greatest Turkish master-builder Mimar Sinan, whose pupils constructed Yugoslavia's most precious mosques: in Plevlja, Čajniče, Višegrad, Sarajevo, Mostar and Foča. This last-named was put up in 1551, and became known as "Aladža", "the Variegated", for its multicoloured striped decoration, previously unknown in this region. The harmony of its outlines, the marble pillars, the fine portal, the cupolas and balconies, and above all, the slender 38-metre minaret, all contribute to make this building the finest pearl in the necklace of Foča's ancient edifices.

The mosque is a foundation of Hasan Čelebija, Bosnian "nazir" i.e. manager, or chief inspector, of the sultan's mines. He was born in a village near Foča, and forcibly taken to Constantinople as a child to become a janissary.

There is a legend that runs as follows: When Čelebija returned to Foča as "nazir" of the sultan's Bosnian, Serbian and Macedonian mines, he met an old woman washing her linen on the bank of the Ćehotina river. She told him her only son had been abducted to Turkey to become a janissary, and she had never heard of him again. Čelebija inquired whether the son had any birthmarks by which he could be recognized. She replied he had worn a mole on his upper arm. When Čelebija rolled up his sleeve and showed her the mark, the old woman, recognizing her son, died on the spot of the shock. On that very location Hasan Čelebija had a mosque built for himself (he is buried just outside the building); for his mother he had an orthodox church raised in her native village, for she had remained a Christian.

There is another legend connected with the construction of the mosque. Master Ramadan is reputed to have simply vanished after he had completed the walls up to the roofing. People were despatched into all the four winds to get hold of him, but could not trace him anywhere. So a whole year passed by — then master Ramadan suddenly reappeared. When Hasan Čelebija wondered where he had strayed, the architect replied: "A year and a day have to pass for the walls of a building to settle — and look, they have settled by a fathom. Only now the roofing can be attempted — that is now one builds for eternity."

Foča's mosque excells for its elegant contours and fanciful interior decoration.

St. Triphon's

Kotor's 800-year-old cathedral is one of the finest Romanesque churches of the Adriatic. Its most precious treasures are the masterpieces of local silversmiths.

St. Triphon's Cathedral (Sv. Tripun), Kotor, is one of the oldest and finest achievements of Romanesque architecture on the Adriatic. It was consecrated on 19th June 1166, in the presence of the Byzantian regent of Dalmatia, the local bishop and numerous other dignitaries. On the same site an earlier church, also dedicated to St. Triphon, had been erected in 809 A.D. by a certain Andrew Saracenis, citizen of Kotor.

In the eight centuries of its existence, the cathedral has suffered various vicissitudes. It was repeatedly damaged by cannon-balls and earthquakes, especially by the disastrous earthquake of 1667, which completely destroyed both bell-towers. They were re-erected in the 17th century in the Baroque style, though retaining their basic Romanesque articulation.